How The West Was Won

THE
WILD WEST

Skyhorse Publishing

How The West Was Won

THE
WILD WEST

BRUCE WEXLER

Skyhorse Publishing

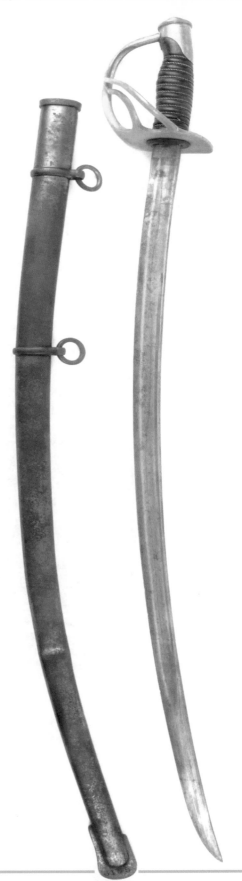

Skyhorse Publishing books may be purchased in bulk at
special discounts for sales promotion, corporate gifts,
fund-raising, or educational purposes. Special editions can
also be created to specifications. For details, contact the
Special Sales Department, Skyhorse Publishing,
307 West 36th Street, 11th Floor, New York, NY 10018 or
"mailto:info@skyhorsepublishing.com"info@skyhorsepublishing.com.

Skyhorse® and Skyhorse Publishing® are registered
trademarks of Skyhorse Publishing, Inc.®,
a Delaware corporation.

www.skyhorsepublishing.com

10 9 8 7 6 5 4 3 2 1

Library of Congress Cataloging-in-Publication Data TK

ISBN: 978-1-61608-437-0

Printed in China

Contents

Introduction

But the West of the old times, with its strong characters, its stern battles, and its tremendous stretches of loneliness, can never be blotted from my mind.

— Buffalo Bill

The West is color. Its colors are animal rather than vegetable, the colors of earth and sunlight and ripeness.

— Jessamyn West

Only remember, west of the Mississippi it's a little more look, see, act. A little less rationalize, comment, talk.

— F. Scott Fitzgerald

Opposite page: Monument Valley, Utah. The dramatic red color of the buttes is derived from iron oxide deposits exposed in the weathered siltstone. This iconic western landscape appears in many movies, including John Ford's *Stagecoach* and *The Searchers*.

America without the West in unthinkable, but its assimilation into the nation was by no means inevitable. The integration of the West into the United States took over a hundred years to complete. The chronicle of this epic achievement is the story of every settler that made it to the region, those that died on the way, and even those that left it empty-handed. It is also the story of the original peoples of the West, the Native Americans, who paid such a devastating price for its settlement.

The legend of the West is woven from the lives of millions of rugged individualists, who made their way there to live freely. It is a fantastic drama with countless players: farmers, preachers, saloon girls, prostitutes, ladies, businessmen, gunslingers, lawmen, Mormons, gamblers, trappers, ranchers, medicine men, and cowboys.

Without a doubt, the most fascinating period in the history of the Western frontier is the century between 1800 and 1900. This was the era of the Old West, and a time of fundamental change. During this time, the West evolved from a wild and untamed territory into an integral part of the modern world. From being virtually uninhabited, apart from the nomadic tribes, the West became somewhere that Americans could put down roots in their own land. Some Westerners became rich beyond the dreams of avarice, while others scratched out the toughest living imaginable from the virgin terrain. Others went completely to the bad, and preyed on their fellow settlers. But even the criminal element of the Old West was somehow larger than life, and more fascinating, and has left a legacy of extraordinary stories.

N. C. Wyeth's atmospheric painting of a stagecoach holdup. He depicts a gentleman bandit asking the passengers for their valuables.

The history of the West is packed with an infinite variety of human experience, which has left a huge impression on the region. As well as mass migration, the nineteenth century also saw the indissoluble linking of the Atlantic and Pacific coasts. Connected in turn by the pioneer trail, the stagecoach, the Pony Express, the railroads, and the telegraph wire, a single nation was gradually forged from two distinct regions. But just as progress pulled the nation together, it also spelled the end of a valuable way of life that had existed unchanged for thousands of years. A human price was paid for every gain.

With the benefit of our modern sensibilities, we can acknowledge that this century of change was one of the most explosive in the nation's history, especially that of the West. As well as bravery, ingenuity, and determination, the nineteenth century witnessed violence, genocide, and environmental disaster.

In the past, the story of the West was told as a string of simple triumphs: the defeat of the Indians, the building of the railroad, the taming of the region by white settlement. Predictably, this was followed by a revisionist backlash spotlighting the dark side of westward expansion: the murder of the native peoples, the decimation of the region's wildlife and natural resources, the triumph of mighty capital over the plucky individual. Today, we seem to have a more balanced view of the complexities of Western integration, while appreciating the mythology of the West and its timeless appeal.

If America has changed the West, the West in its turn has had a massive impact on America. When the United States became a continental nation, it was transformed into a far bigger and more powerful country with greater resources of every kind. The West has also permeated the very fabric of American cultural life. Its wild and beautiful landscape is familiar to millions of people who have never breathed its free air. Through its portrayal in the movies, literature, television, fashion, and even toys, the West has become a familiar concept. It has come to represent the very best of America itself: freedom, courage, and self-determination. It is both a unique part of America, and a metaphor for the country as a whole.

With all its mixed bag of courage, violence, creativity, and exploitation, the West has a compelling charm to almost all Americans and to millions of people in the world at large.

To anyone with an interest in the Old West, *The West* is a virtual tour of the most extraordinary century in the region's history. The book recreates its drama, iconography, atmosphere, and its cavalcade of legendary characters.

Native Americans in the West

Opposite page: Magnificent regalia of pierced shells, ermine, and feathers.

Native Americans first came to America around forty thousand years ago over the frozen Bering Strait, known as Beringia, which formed a land bridge between Siberia and Alaska. These people came from Asia, and were of Mongolian origin. The abundant livestock of their new homeland sustained these new

Above: White settlers began to arrive in North America in the sixteenth century and immediately began to influence the native tribes.

Americans, and attracted further immigrants. They arrived in waves, and pushed the earlier incomers further and further east and south until the entire continent was thinly populated. When the first white settlers arrived, there were around ten million Native Americans in America. The tribes had hugely diverse cultures and lifestyles, and a complicated oral and pictorial culture. Some were hunter-gatherers.

Right: Sauk chief Black Hawk. Black Hawk did not believe in ownership of land, and fought to maintain tribal traditions.

Opposite page: The nomadic tribes of the Great Plains used teepees winter and summer. This one is covered in buffalo hide.

Others were farmers. Many had long traditions of producing exquisite artifacts from natural materials. It was Christopher Columbus who coined the term "Indian" for these peoples, under the misapprehension that he had reached the Indies. It was actually San Salvador on which he landed in 1492. The new white settlers had a devastating effect on the indigenous population. The European diseases they carried (typhus, smallpox, influenza, measles, and diphtheria) infected and killed

as many as ninety-five percent of them. Perhaps the one positive consequence of the incoming Conquistadors was the introduction of horses to America. This had a huge impact on life on the Great Plains, enabling the Native Americans to kill buffalo and other game far more effectively. It also led to the invention of the travois to move their camps and possessions more quickly and easily, by dragging them along the ground. Horses were also used in inter-tribal warfare.

The completely opposing beliefs held by the white settlers and the Native Americans soon became a source of conflict. The indigenous people were nomadic, and believed that the man belonged to the earth, not the other way around. By complete contrast, the Europeans were bound by the conventions of property ownership, and had a settled, cooperative style of living, and organized religion. This gulf between beliefs was well put by the famous Sauk chief, Black Hawk,

Above: Apache scouts, armed with rifles. They were photographed in Arizona in 1871.

speaking in 1831. "My reason tells me that land cannot be sold; nothing can be sold but such things as can be carried away." As more and more white settlers arrived, the process of American settlement began again. European settlers arrived in the East, and gradually pushed the Native Americans further and further west.

Completely out-gunned by the white Americans' superior weapons, the Indian stood no chance against them. Although different problems sparked conflict between the races, the Indian Wars were fought over land rights. The United States government believed that buffalo-hunting Plains tribes were preventing white settlement across swathes of western territory, including Kansas, Nebraska, the Dakotas, Montana, Wyoming, and Colorado. It was generally believed that the Indians were hindering the "Manifest Destiny" of white people to "overspread the continent." President Andrew Jackson set out the agenda of the U.S. Government in the Indian Removal Act of 1830. Many Americans held the same view as General William Sherman, who asserted, "All Indians who are not on reservations are hostile, and will remain so until killed off."

Native Americans saw things completely differently. The famous Sioux chief and negotiator, Spotted Tail, countered, "This war did not spring up on our land, this war was brought by the children of the Great Father." The first of these land wars was the Arikara War of 1823. The Arikara tribe were semi-nomadic farmers living in South Dakota who were attacked by the Sioux and the U.S. Army (under the leadership of Col. Henry Leavenworth) and driven into the North of the state. The conflict set the tone for many future encounters. The Indian Wars rumbled on for decades, and encompassed hundreds of attacks, fights, and skirmishes between the Native Americans, settlers, and the U.S. Army. The most devastating period of hostilities took place between 1866 and 1890. Geographically, the conflict spread over most of the western states: Arizona, California, Colorado, Montana, North Dakota, Oklahoma, South Dakota, Texas, Utah, Washington, and Wyoming.

Opposite page: Arikara warrior Bear's Belly, wearing a grizzly bearskin. The Arikara were close cousins of the Pawnee, and were a nomadic and agricultural tribe.

Above: A necklace of eagle talons that belonged to Rough Hair.

Overleaf: A map showing the distribution of the Native American tribes before westward expansion.

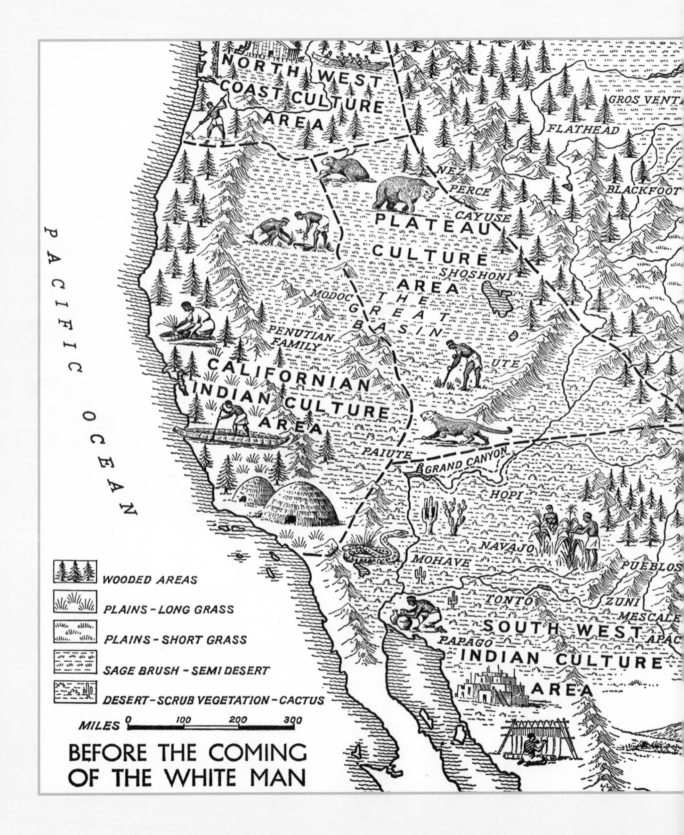

PACIFIC OCEAN

NORTH WEST COAST CULTURE AREA

GROS VENT

FLATHEAD

NEZ PERCE

BLACKFOOT

CAYUSE

PLATEAU CULTURE AREA

SHOSHONI

THE GREAT BASIN

MODOC

PENUTIAN FAMILY

UTE

CALIFORNIAN INDIAN CULTURE AREA

PAIUTE

GRAND CANYON

HOPI

NAVAJO

PUEBLOS

MOHAVE

ZUNI

MESCALE

TONTO

SOUTH WEST INDIAN CULTURE AREA

APAC

PAPAGO

WOODED AREAS

PLAINS – LONG GRASS

PLAINS – SHORT GRASS

SAGE BRUSH – SEMI DESERT

DESERT – SCRUB VEGETATION – CACTUS

MILES 0   100   200   300

BEFORE THE COMING OF THE WHITE MAN

There were many famous battles and countless attacks, but the Indian tribes scored very few serious hits against their white opponents. One of their few victories was at Custer's Last Stand. Far more common were massacres of the tribespeople, like that perpetrated at Wounded Knee in South Dakota, and terrible treatment, such as the infamous Trail of Tears. The Trail of Tears was the forced removal of the Cherokee Nation from Georgia to Oklahoma, under the terms of the New Echota Treaty of 1835. A string of forts was built along the route to corral the Indians and protect the troops who forced the thousand-mile march to the West. The sophisticated Cherokees, who had been so tolerant of the white settlers arriving to

Above: Comanche chief Quanah Parker. Parker was the son of Chief Peta Nocona and Cynthia Ann Parker, who had been captured by the tribe at the age of nine.

Right: A Navajo mother and child wearing traditional silver and turquoise jewelry.

Opposite page: This beaded buckskin jacket was produced by Lakota Sioux craftspeople in around 1890.

Opposite page: Chief Geronimo was a Chiricahua Apache who fought the Apache Wars to preserve tribal lands. He surrendered in 1886, and died in 1909.

share their homeland, were herded like animals and died by the thousands, particularly during the savagely cold winter of 1838 to 1839. Among the victims was Quatie, the wife of tribal chief John Ross, who died just outside Little Rock.

Estimates of casualties in the Indian Wars vary, but a reasonable approximation would probably be around forty-five thousand Indians and nineteen thousand whites. These casualties included many women and children on both sides, many

Right: A Navajo war captain. He wears a war hat of tanned leather, and carries a lance and rawhide shield.

of whom perished in bloodthirsty massacres. Both sides were extremely violent and destructive. Despite this, remnants of the native inhabitants survived, but they account for only around two percent of the modern population of the United States. The descendants of over five hundred different tribes endure, but most have lost their distinctive languages and culture.

Even a brief analysis of a few of the most prominent tribal groupings gives an insight into the great variety of traditions and lifestyle.

Opposite page: A painting by John Hauser Jr. depicts Sioux Chief Iron Tail wearing his spectacular war bonnet (below). He was a survivor of the Wounded Knee Massacre.

APACHE

Apache is the Zuni word for "enemy," but the Apache called themselves the Dine, "the people" in their Athapascan language. The Apache were the major tribe of the American Southwest. Made up from nine distinct sub-tribes, they populated Arizona, New Mexico, Oklahoma, and Texas. Related to the Navajo and enjoying a similar way of life, their tribal deity was known as Yusan or Ussen. Despite a fairly unsettled lifestyle, the tribe often lived in wooden huts or adobe structures rather than under canvas. They had a reputation for being fierce warriors. They had enthusiastically adopted horses from the Spanish invaders, and were experts in horsemanship, using the animals for both hunting and raiding other tribes. Geronimo was one of the most famous Apache chiefs. His capture in 1886 was hugely symbolic, and signaled the end of the Apache warrior culture. In fact, they were the last tribe to surrender to the United States government.

COMANCHE

The word "Comanche" comes from the Spanish phrase *camino ancho*, meaning "wide trail." Their mother tongue is derived from Aztec and is related to the languages of the Shoshone, Ute, and Paiute. Originally from the Rocky Mountains, the Comanche moved onto the Plains to hunt buffalo, and became a nomadic tribe. The tribe emerged as a distinct group before 1700, when they broke away from the Shoshone tribe. The Comanche existed in dozens of autonomous groups, and expanded by capturing women and children from rival groups and assimilating them. The horse was pivotal to their lifestyle, and the Comanche introduced the animal to other people of the Plains. They had originally used dogs to pull their travois, but moved to using horses. The Comanche people had a traditional division of labor; the men hunted and

fought, while the women brought up the children, cooked the food, and made clothes from buckskin, deerskin, buffalo hide, bearskin, and wolf skin. The tribe tended not to eat fish or fowl, preferring game meat flavored with berries, nuts, honey, and tallow. The Comanche were a very hospitable tribe who worshiped the Great Spirit. The tribe was run by a council of ministers, which included both a "peace chief" and a "war chief." Medicine men were also influential; their duties included naming children. The Comanche were indulgent parents who cherished their progeny. Retired warriors gathered daily in the smoke lodge.

Unfortunately, like many other Native Americans, the tribe fell victim to European diseases such as smallpox and cholera. Their population crashed from twenty thousand people in the mid-1800's to a few thousand by the 1870's. By the 1860s, many Comanche were confined to reservations. Their condition had deteriorated dramatically. The buffalo was virtually extinct, and their skirmishes with the U.S. Army had been devastating.

Above: Jenny LaPointe made these Lakota Sioux moccasins. They date from around 1900. Jenny LaPointe was a member of Buffalo Bill's *Wild West Show*.

Opposite page: Ahfitche, the governor of San Felipe Pueblo, New Mexico uses a drill to make holes in shells for use in jewelry. The photograph was taken in 1880.

Right: This rawhide dance rattle belonged to Crazy Crow, a member of the Plains Crow tribe.

CHEROKEE

The Cherokee were one of the largest tribes of the Southeast, known as the "Tsalagi" in their own language. Cherokee comes from the Creek word for "people of a different speech." They had migrated from the Northwest following defeats by the Iroquois and Delaware. They became a settled agricultural people, who lived in around two hundred villages. Typically, each of these consisted of between thirty and sixty dwellings, together with a large council house where the sacred fire was kept. The tribe cultivated the "three sisters" of corn, beans, and squash. They were also hunter-gatherers, with a highly sophisticated standard of living. The Cherokee were heavily influenced by white settlers, and invented their own written language consisting of eighty-six characters in 1821. The Cherokee also traded with the British. But a devastating smallpox epidemic in 1753 killed half the tribe. They also fell out with their British allies and, in 1760, the Cherokee warriors massacred the garrison at Fort Loudon in eastern Tennessee.

Trying to protect their valuable lands from white settlement, the tribe sold the land of other tribes. An honest Cherokee chief took Daniel Boone aside and told him, "We have sold you much fine land, but I am afraid you will have trouble if you try to live there." But fighting between the tribe and white settlers continued unabated, exacerbated when gold was discovered on their lands. The Indian Removal Act of 1821 stripped the Cherokee of any legal rights, and they became the victim of every kind of theft and violence. They were finally driven to surrender their homelands in return for $5,000,000 and seven million acres of land in Oklahoma. But the treaty proved to be a fraud. The Cherokee were driven out of their lands by force, and embarked on the infamous Trail of Tears. Many died of measles, whooping cough, and dysentery, while others perished from exposure. In the end, they were forced to abandon even the Oklahoma territory they had been awarded. The tribe was finally compensated by the U.S. government in 1961 with a payment of $15 million.

Opposite page: Sioux warrior Yellow Shirt holds a sacred horse dance stick in his right hand. In his left, he holds a beaded pipe and a tobacco bag.

THE NAVAJO

The Navajo remain the largest Native American tribe, with around two hundred thousand surviving members. Navajo comes from the Spanish for "people with big lands." The tribe called themselves the "Dine" or "people." They originally came from Northwest Canada and Alaska, but traveled to the Southwest part of America. The tribe grew corn, beans, squash, and melons and wove attractive rugs and fabrics. The Navajo lived in fairly substantial circular dwellings called *hogans*, made from wooden poles, tree bark, and mud. Traditionally, the doors always opened to the east. When the white settlers arrived, the tribe stole their sheep and horses and integrated both animals into their tribal lives. The Navajo nation now extends into Utah, Arizona, and New Mexico. It extends over twenty-seven thousand square miles, and is larger than several U.S. states.

Opposite page: A Cheyenne warrior wears a war bonnet crafted with ermine drops and a beaded brow band. His sash is decorated with a star motif.

THE SIOUX

"Sioux" is the name given to the tribe by French fur traders who had close relations with them in the late seventeenth century. It was the traders' diminutive of the tribe's Indian name, "Nadouessioux," or "the adders." The tribe was a large and disparate racial group, composed of three distinct ethnic strains. The Sioux migrated to the Plains in the late eighteenth century, and substantially changed their way of life from being canoe men and gatherers of wild rice to horse-riding hunters. Largely through trading with the French, many Sioux braves also became armed with guns. The Sioux involved themselves in many struggles with other tribes, but also began to attack settlers to the area. The "Minnesota outbreak" of 1862 resulted in widespread Sioux violence, and several hundred settlers were brutally murdered. A court marshal condemned three hundred tribesmen to hang for their part in the killing spree, but President Lincoln spared all but thirty-eight. Despite this, the resulting hanging at Mankato, Minnesota, remains the largest mass execution in American history. A vicious cycle

Above: Sioux Chief Hollow Horn Bear, who as a young man fought with Sitting Bull at the Battle of Little Bighorn.

Opposite Page: Hunkpapa Lakota Sioux tribal chief Sitting Bull routed Custer's Seventh Cavalry at the Battle of the Little Bighorn. Later, he appeared in Bill Cody's *Wild West Show*.

Left: Red Cloud was the head chief of the Oglala Lakota Sioux. Between 1866 and 1868, he waged Red Cloud's War, fighting for control over traditional tribal lands in Powder River Country. He died in the Pine Ridge Reservation, South Dakota, in 1909.

of murder and revenge continued. Red Cloud's War raged for two years starting in 1866. Subsequent hostilities broke out in the Black Hills, including the killing of Custer and his men. In 1890, the tribe's famous Ghost Dance ritual culminated in more murder and mayhem, and resulted in the death of Sitting Bull as he tried to protect the tribe's independence. This in turn provoked the fight at Wounded Knee Creek against the forces of the U.S. Seventh Cavalry.

Beaten by U.S. government forces, the Sioux were mostly confined to reservations by the end of the nineteenth century. Confined, the tribe reverted to the farming traditions of their past, raising cattle and corn rather than hunting the almost extinct buffalo. Most famous Sioux, including Little Crow, Crazy Horse, Red Cloud, and Sitting Bull were known for their fighting prowess, but the tribe was also noted for its dancing and fine craftwork.

Cavalry Regiments of the Indian Wars

Below: An early cavalryman with a saddle-mounted holster.

Opposite page: William Tecumseh Sherman became Commanding General of the Army in 1869. He waged the Indian Wars for twenty years. His stated objective was the extermination of the Native Americans.

Of all the institutions of the Old West, the cavalry is surely one of the most iconic. From 1865 to 1890, the cavalry played a huge role in western expansion, patrolling the frontier and protecting would-be settlers from Indian attack. Effectively, the frontier started west of the Mississippi River, and as western settlement became increasingly widespread, the cavalry became responsible for a huge area of territory.

The cavalry also became a major enforcer of the civil law in the region, and became involved in many actions to bring lawbreakers and gunmen to justice. A good example of this would be the 1870 shootout between Wild Bill Hickok and riders of the Seventh that took place in Hays, Kansas. Hickok killed one cavalry officer and wounded another.

The role of the cavalry in the post-Civil War period was determined in 1869, when President Grant appointed William Tecumseh Sherman Commanding General of the United States Army and the cavalry also came under his command. At this time, Sherman's major preoccupation was the subjugation of the Indian tribes, which he saw as a barrier to westward expansion. To this end, he created the Plains Cavalry, and recruited an additional four regiments to deal with the so-called "Indian problem." The Indian Wars raged until the Massacre of Wounded Knee in 1890, and became the focus of the Plains Cavalry for over two decades.

Each cavalry regiment consisted of twelve troops of approximately ninety-five men. Although recruiting officers was no problem, as many men stayed in the army when the Civil War ended, it proved much harder to engage ordinary troopers. The ranks became filled with many wanted men and immigrants, not all of whom spoke

Several guns of the period became highly
identified with the U.S. Cavalry in the years
following the Civil War.

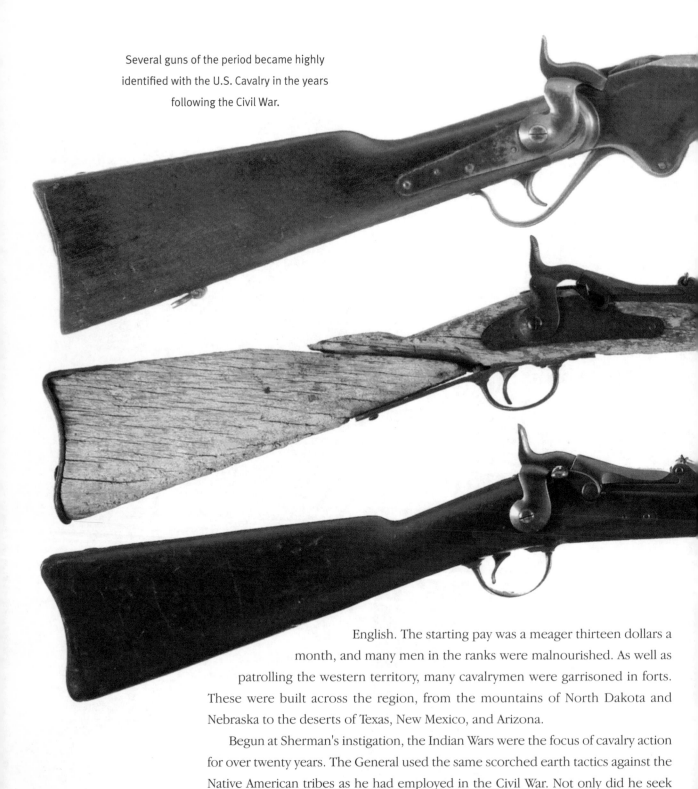

English. The starting pay was a meager thirteen dollars a
month, and many men in the ranks were malnourished. As well as
patrolling the western territory, many cavalrymen were garrisoned in forts.
These were built across the region, from the mountains of North Dakota and
Nebraska to the deserts of Texas, New Mexico, and Arizona.

Begun at Sherman's instigation, the Indian Wars were the focus of cavalry action
for over twenty years. The General used the same scorched earth tactics against the
Native American tribes as he had employed in the Civil War. Not only did he seek
military victory against them, he also wanted to deprive them of their means of

Above: A Model 1865 Spencer carbine. The gun was chambered for the .50 caliber rimfire cartridge. Many Buffalo Soldiers of the Ninth Cavalry stationed at Fort Davis, Texas, were armed with the gun.

Above: A Springfield Model 1873, recovered from the battlefield at Little Bighorn. Custer's Seventh Cavalry were armed with the gun. It was ineffective because the Indian braves rarely came within its range. The gun was nicknamed the "Trapdoor" after its Allin breechloading system.

Above: Standard Model 1873 Springfield carbine. The Springfield was the first standard-issue breech-loading rifle adopted by the United States Army.

survival. In the case of the Plains Indians, this meant the decimation of the buffalo.

The Seventh United States Cavalry was undoubtedly the most famous regiment to fight in the Indian Wars. Constituted in 1866, the regiment was made up of twelve companies, or "troops." Like most of the post-war cavalry, its troopers were armed mainly with single-action Colt .45 revolvers and modified single-shot .50 caliber Model 1865 Spencer carbines. These were based on the Spencer Model 1863 of the early Civil War era, but had shorter, twenty-inch barrels. These guns were finally replaced by the Springfield Model 1873. Although sabers were still issued, these were now largely ceremonial.

Above: The single-action Colt .45 revolver was adopted by the U.S. Cavalry in the postbellum era. It became known as "the gun that won the West."

Until 1871, the Seventh was based at Fort Riley in Kansas. Its mission was to enforce United States law in the subjugated South. But the regiment was also involved in anti-Indian action, including the famous 1868 Battle of Washita River. Commanded by General Custer, the 7th attacked Chief Black Kettle's Cheyenne village. Even at the time, Custer's attack on a sleeping village was controversial. The general was accused of sadism, and his men of killing women and children.

In 1873, the Seventh U.S. Cavalry moved its base to Fort Abraham

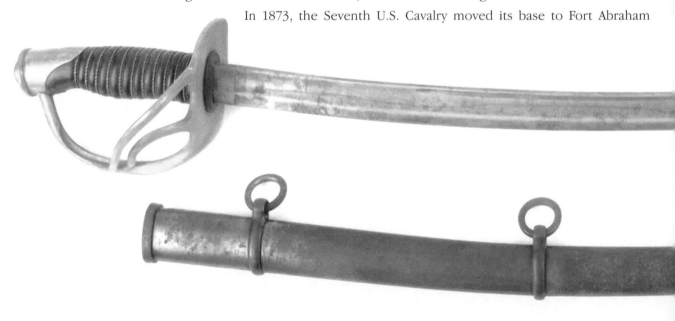

Lincoln, in Dakota Territory. The regiment's initial brief was to reconnoiter and map the Black Hills mountain range, which stretches between South Dakota and Wyoming. Custer's discovery of gold in the Black Hills, during his expedition of 1874, had a profound effect on the region. Not only did this discovery precipitate the huge social upheaval of the Gold Rush, but it also exacerbated conflict with the Sioux, Lakota, and Cheyenne tribes, who were under the leadership of Sitting Bull and Crazy Horse. Modern historians accuse President Grant of deliberately provoking war with the native peoples; he was desperate for gold-fuelled growth to lift the economy out of depression.

But victory against the Sioux and Cheyenne peoples was only achieved at a huge cost to the men of the Seventh Cavalry. The Battle of the Little Bighorn (June 25–26, 1876), also known as Custer's Last Stand, saw two hundred and sixty-eight cavalrymen killed, and a further sixty wounded. The death toll included Custer himself and two of his brothers – Captain Thomas Custer, and their youngest brother, civilian scout and forage master Boston Custer – and Custer's nephew, Autie Reed. Not only were the cavalry outnumbered by two thousand braves at Little Bighorn, but they were also out-gunned. The U.S. forces were armed with newly issued single-shot Springfield rifles, while many of the Indians had various repeating rifles and carbines such as Henrys, Winchesters, and Spencers. Custer's Last Stand became the most serious defeat inflicted on the cavalry in the Plains Wars. Every man and horse of the Seventh cavalry that fought at Little Bighorn perished at the scene; the single exception was Captain Keogh's famous mount, Comanche.

Below: A cavalry saber from the Indian Wars period, made by Ames.

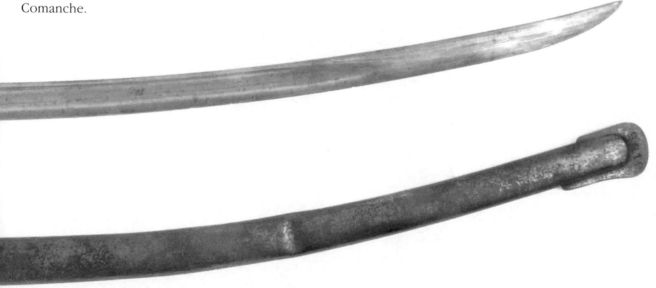

Opposite page: George Armstrong Custer was one of the most famous cavalry commanders in the Indian Wars. He met his demise at the Battle of the Little Bighorn of 1876 at the hands of a combined force of Lakota, Northern Cheyenne, and Arapaho Indians.

Left: Custer meets with his Crow scouts. His favorite Remington rifle rests on the guy rope.

Despite his complete failure, General Custer's reputation remained strangely unstained by this terrible defeat, largely due to the efforts of his widow, Elizabeth Bacon Custer, and friend, Buffalo Bill Cody.

Several other United States Cavalry regiments fought in the Indian Wars. The Fourth United States Cavalry was formed in 1855, and was deployed to Texas after the war. Its duties were to protect settlers and the U.S. mail from Indian attack. In 1871 the regiment was called to more active duties, protecting the Texas frontier from Comanche and Kiowa attack. In March 1873, a large part of the regiment was transferred to Fort Clark, from where they made forays into Mexico to prevent highly destructive Apache raids into Texas. In 1880, the Fourth was transferred to Arizona

Above: Custer's Seventh Cavalry unit on their way to Little Bighorn.
Opposite page: Indian chief with Winchester Trapper carbine.

Territory, where they continued to pursue their nemesis, the Apache. Six years later, in 1886, the Fourth was instrumental in the capture of Geronimo. In 1890, the troops of the Fourth were redeployed to Washington State, and took no further part in the Indian Wars. Over the period of their involvement, the regiment had had many successes against a number of Indian tribes, such as the Comanche (including the Quahadi and Kotsoteka Comanche), Kiowa, Cheyenne, and Apache tribes.

Top: Custer's Last Stand. Armed with single shot Springfield carbines, his forces were outgunned by the Indian attackers.

Bottom: The dreadful scene after the Battle of Little Bighorn.

Opposite page: Custer attired in his cavalry uniform of fringed buckskin.

The Fifth United States Cavalry was formed in Louisville, Kentucky, in 1855, and was originally designated the Second United States Cavalry Regiment. In 1861, this regiment split between men loyal to the Confederacy and those who supported the Union. The Union cavalrymen were re-designated as the Fifth, and these men were instrumental in saving their artillery at the Battle of Gaines' Mill in 1862. In the post-bellum Plains Indian Wars, the regiment's main duty was to recapture escaped Sioux and Cheyenne and repatriate them to their reservations. They were also instrumental in the defeat of the Miniconjou Sioux at the Battle of Slim Buttes, which took place 1876 in Dakota Territory. Colonel Wesley Merritt led the troops in this engagement. This victory was of huge psychological importance, as it was the first significant defeat of the tribes since the annihilation of Custer's Seventh.

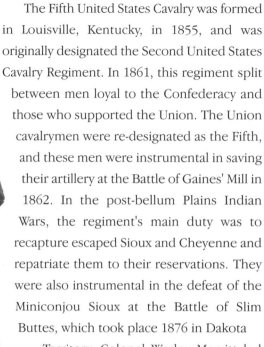

The Sixth United States Cavalry, also known as the "Fighting Sixth" also took a major part in the Indian Wars. It was raised in 1861, and became part of the Union Army of the Potomac during the Civil War. Between 1865 and 1871, the regiment was deployed to Texas during Reconstruction. The regiment also fought in the Indian Wars, and clashed with Geronimo and his Apache braves on more than one occasion.

The Eigth Cavalry Regiment was formed in 1866, and organized at Camp Reynolds, in Angel, California. Unsurprisingly,

many of its recruits were disappointed "forty-niners," and were reputed to be pretty wild characters. The regiment's first duties were to protect the settlers and travelers of Nevada, Colorado, Arizona, and New Mexico from opportunistic attacks from Apache and Navajo tribesmen. They often provided armed escorts. The Eigth also fought in the Apache Wars of southern New Mexico, and engaged with warriors from the Navajo, Comanche, and Kiowa tribes. As more settlers moved into the

Above: The Sixth U.S. Cavalry training their horses at Fort Bayard, New Mexico. Opposite page: A saddle-mounted carbine boot for the 1873 Springfield.

Above: Custer's favorite gun, a .50 caliber Remington single shot rifle.
Custer wrote to Remington praising the gun.

Left: The Sixth U.S. Cavalry practice saber exercise at Fort Bayard. The Fort was established in 1866 to protect miners and settlers along the Apache Trail.

Right: The Seventh Cavalry surrounded the Indian camp at Wounded Knee Creek with four of these Hotchkiss guns.

Below: The aftermath of the Wounded Knee Massacre that took place on December 29, 1890.

Northwestern states, the Eigth also undertook the longest-ever cavalry march in May, 1885. The march was two-thousand six-hundred miles long, to their two new regimental headquarters at Fort Meade, South Dakota, and Fort Keogh, Montana.

The involvement of the cavalry regiments in the Indian Wars ended in 1890 with the Massacre of Wounded Knee. During this period, the cavalry had mounted many protective operations for the people of the West, but had also been an instrument of United States Government policy. As well as facilitating the settling and civilizing of the western territories, their role had also included the dispossession and subjugation of the native peoples of the region.

Above: At least one-hundred and fifty men, women, and children of the Lakota Sioux tribe were killed at Wounded Knee. Another fifty people were wounded. Many of the casualties were fatally injured.

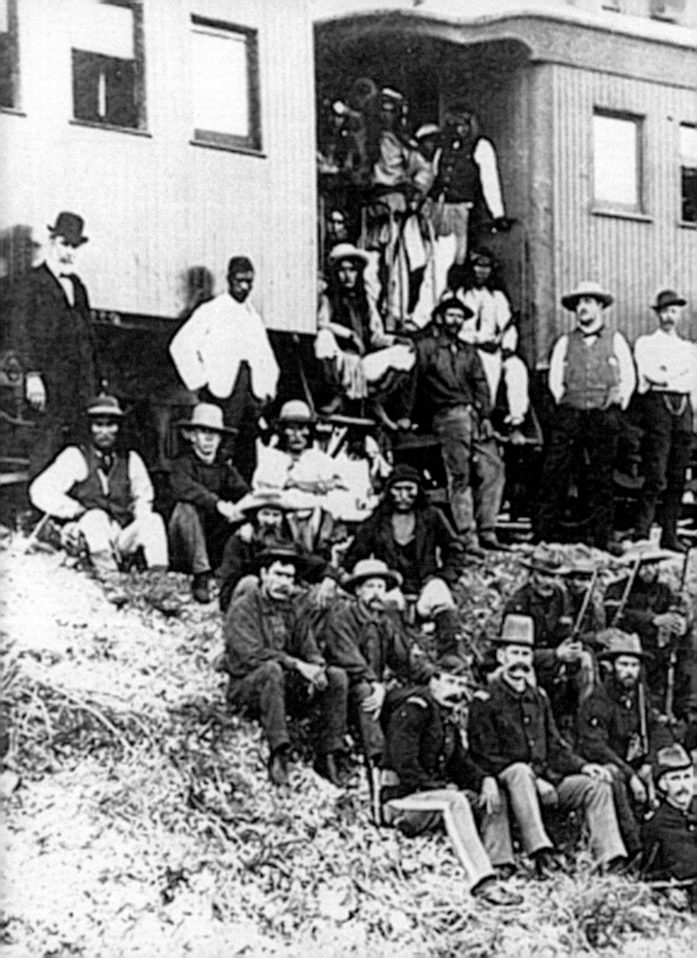

Left: Captured Apache warriors (including Geronimo) surrounded by cavalrymen. Geronimo gave himself up to First Lieutenant Charles B. Gatewood, but officially surrendered to General Nelson A. Miles on September 4, 1886 at Skeleton Canyon, Arizona.

Winchester 1873

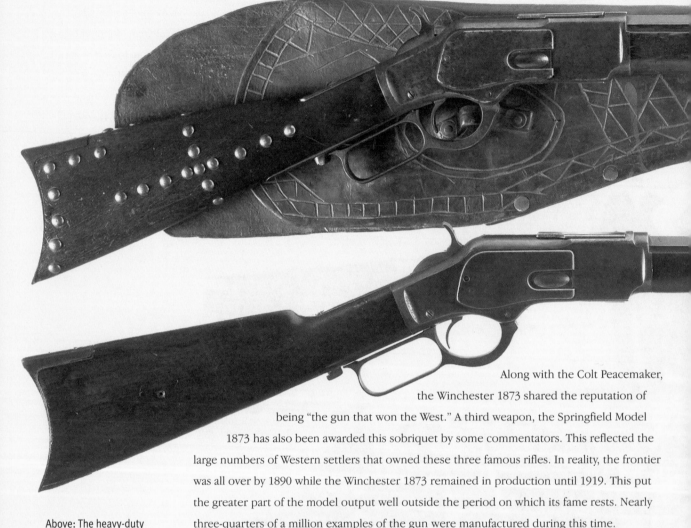

Above: The heavy-duty steel frame and receiver enables the 1873 to use heavier centerfire ammunition.

Along with the Colt Peacemaker, the Winchester 1873 shared the reputation of being "the gun that won the West." A third weapon, the Springfield Model 1873 has also been awarded this sobriquet by some commentators. This reflected the large numbers of Western settlers that owned these three famous rifles. In reality, the frontier was all over by 1890 while the Winchester 1873 remained in production until 1919. This put the greater part of the model output well outside the period on which its fame rests. Nearly three-quarters of a million examples of the gun were manufactured during this time.

Horace Smith and Daniel Wesson formed the Volcanic Repeating Arms Company in 1855, in Norwich, Connecticut. Volcanic moved to New Haven, Connecticut in 1856, but the firm had become insolvent by the end of the year. Oliver Winchester purchased the bankrupt company and re-launched it as the New Haven Arms Company in April, 1857. After the Civil War, the company was re-named again, this time as the Winchester Repeating Arms Company. The first Winchester rifle, the Model 1866 was launched that year. It was a repeating rifle that could fire a number of shots before it needed to be reloaded. The Model 1873 was a steel-framed version of the earlier gun, lighter than the earlier brass-framed model. Gone was its pretty "yellow boy" appearance. Its extra strength also meant that the rifle could use more

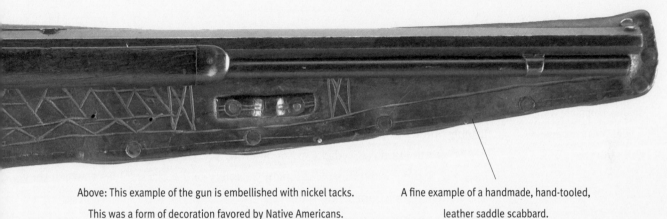

Above: This example of the gun is embellished with nickel tacks. This was a form of decoration favored by Native Americans.

A fine example of a handmade, hand-tooled, leather saddle scabbard.

powerful .44-40 inch centerfire cartridges. Each bullet was propelled by a cartridge that contained forty grains of black powder, which gave the Winchester excellent stopping-power. The popularity of the gun led Colt to manufacture a version of their famous Peacemaker chambered for the same powerful round. This meant that their ammunition was interchangeable, and a man only needed to carry one kind of cartridge.

Winchester produced three variants of the Model 1873: the rifle, carbine, and musket. The rifle version had a twenty-four inch barrel, while the carbine barrel was only twenty inches. This meant that the carbine became the most popular variant of the gun, because it was the most portable.

In 1950, Jimmy Stewart starred in the Anthony Mann movie, *Winchester '73*, which was inspired by the legend of this popular weapon. The character of Wyatt Earp also makes an appearance in the movie. Stewart's character, Lin McAdam, wins a Winchester rifle in a shooting contest by shooting through a tiny stamp. The film is set in 1876, and the shooting competition takes place just as the news of

Custer's Last Stand is spreading across the West. The movie was so successful that it was credited with reviving interest in antique firearms.

SPECIFICATIONS

Caliber: 0.44-40 inch

Length of barrel: 24 inches

Barrel shape: octagonal

Finish: blue/casehardened

Action: 15 shot lever action

Year of manufacture: 1890

Manufacturer: Winchester Repeating Arms Company, New Haven, Connecticut

Buffalo Soldiers

Opposite page: An immaculately-dressed African-American buffalo soldier, complete with bugle. The photograph dates from the 1870s.

African-American soldiers formed a significant part of the United States Cavalry in the post-bellum period. They became widely known as the "Buffalo Soldiers." "Colored" regiments were constituted by a July 1866 Act of Congress, which set out how segregated regiments would "increase and fix the Current Peace Establishment of the United States."

The term "Buffalo Soldiers" was coined by the Cheyenne tribe in 1867. It was inspired by their admiration of the fighting ability of the black soldiers, which they said matched the courage and stamina of the buffalo. The term was also a reference to the men's close cropped, curly black hair. There were four buffalo regiments; two cavalry (the ninth and the tenth), and two infantry (the Twenty-fourth and the Twenty-fifth). These soldiers became the first African-American soldiers to be recruited to the United States Army in peacetime. The men were mostly freed slaves, and many were Civil War veterans. Over one-hundred and eighty thousand black men had fought for the Union, and thirty-three thousand had fallen. These African-American soldiers were highly motivated by a desire for respect and for recognition of their first-rate soldiering. They won great admiration for their courage, and eighteen black combatants received the Congressional Medal of Honor for their part in the Civil War. These men wore the "Buffalo Soldiers" tag with pride.

Ironically, strict segregation meant that black soldiers constructed many forts and facilities that they were forbidden to use. Ultimately the Buffalo Soldiers formed twenty percent of the post-war cavalry and fought a hundred and seventy-seven engagements in the Indian Wars. Thirteen enlisted men and six officers from the Buffalo regiments won the Medal of Honor during this period. During the decades of the Indian Wars, the Buffalo Soldiers' uniform consisted of a flannel shirt worn under a dark blue blouse, light blue trousers tucked into over-the-knee boots, and a kepi cap decorated with the crossed saber and their regimental motto. The motto of the ninth was "Ready and Forward." That of the tenth was "We Can, We Will." When mounted, the cavalrymen wore a slouch campaign hat. Initially these were black, but became grayish-brown after 1874. Although the Buffalo Soldiers were not issued with regulation neckerchiefs, these were vital to protect them from the dust of the Plains, so most wore their own. These were usually yellow, red, or white. Like their white counterparts, the Buffalo Soldiers were armed with Springfield carbine rifles, Colt Single-Action Army Revolvers (Model 1873) in .45 caliber, and traditional cavalry sabers.

Above: A group of Buffalo Soldiers pose for a casual photograph.

The army's black cavalry and infantry regiments numbered around five thousand men, and formed at least ten percent of the soldiers who guarded the Western Frontier, which ran between Montana and Arizona. This duty lasted for a quarter of a century, between the end of the Civil War and the end of the Indian Wars (1891). By this time, the West was considered to have been "won."

Day-to-day life for Buffalo Soldiers was tough. Their rations were limited to beef, bacon, potatoes, beans, and a few fresh vegetables, with fruit or jam as an irregular treat. The men were on duty for seven days a week, with only the Fourth of July and Christmas Day given as holidays. Their living conditions were also grim, during the early post-Civil War years, most of their barracks were little better than dilapidated huts, poorly ventilated and full of vermin. These unhyginic surroundings led to outbreaks of dysentery, bronchitis, and diarrhea. Despite this, morale and standards of military discipline remained very high in the black regiments. When on duty, the men were drilled, paraded, and inspected regularly. They were also noted for the great pride they took in their uniforms.

On the positive side, Buffalo Soldiers were often offered a rudimentary education, and their poor living conditions were broadly similar to those endured by their white counterparts.

The Ninth U.S. Cavalry regiment was raised in July 1866, at the instigation of General Phillip Sheridan, as a segregated African-American unit. It was raised in Louisville, Kentucky, and consisted largely of men who had fought on the Union side during the Civil War. They were paid a salary of $13 per month, with their living expenses covered. The regime placed under the command of Colonel Edward Hatch. In June 1867, the regiment was ordered to Texas, charged with protecting the stage and mail routes, building and maintaining forts in the area, and establishing the civil law. The regiment was also involved in the famous Battle of Beecher Island, which took place in Colorado. Answering a call for help from Colorado's acting governor, Frank Hall, fifty handpicked men overpowered a combined force of over six hundred warriors from the Arapaho, Cheyenne, Brule, and Oglala Sioux tribes. The regiment suffered only six fatalities.

Between 1875 and 1881, the Ninth became increasingly involved in the Apache Wars. Their distinguished service included the heroic Battle of Tularosa, where

Left: A highly-decorated group of Buffalo Soldiers from the Tenth Cavalry Regiment.

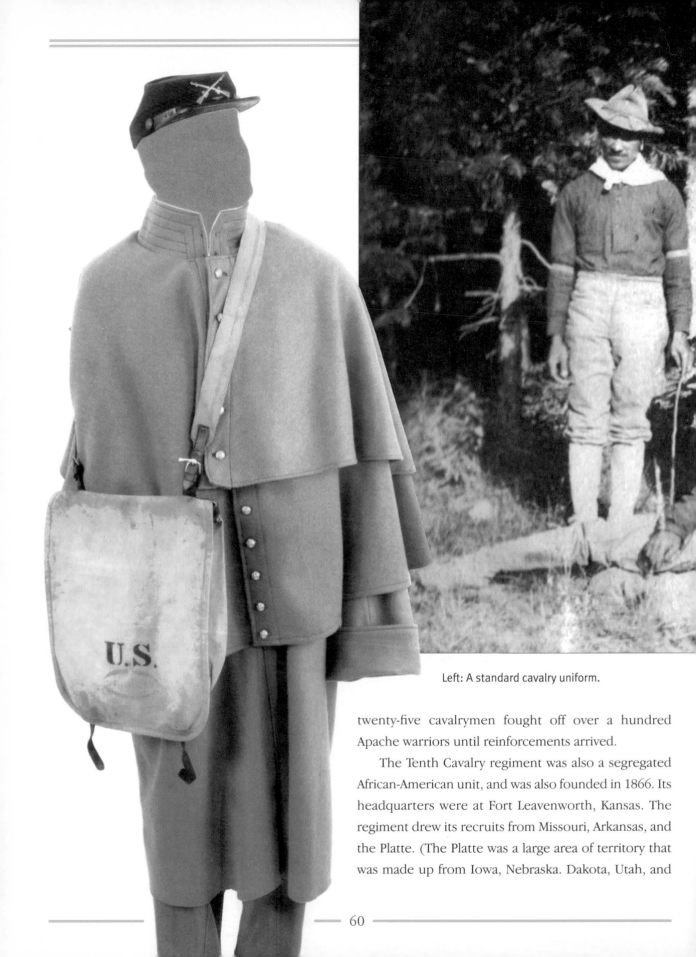

Left: A standard cavalry uniform.

twenty-five cavalrymen fought off over a hundred Apache warriors until reinforcements arrived.

The Tenth Cavalry regiment was also a segregated African-American unit, and was also founded in 1866. Its headquarters were at Fort Leavenworth, Kansas. The regiment drew its recruits from Missouri, Arkansas, and the Platte. (The Platte was a large area of territory that was made up from Iowa, Nebraska. Dakota, Utah, and

Idaho.) The men of the Tenth Cavalry were of a notoriously high caliber. The regiment was led by white officers, and led by Civil War hero Benjamin Henry Grierson. Grierson had a great belief in the black soldiers he had recruited. For the next eight years, his men were based at several different forts in Kansas and Oklahoma. Their duties included protecting railway workers as they built the Kansas and Pacific railroad (between Kansas City and Denver). The railroad had a huge impact on the life of the West, and greatly increased the flow of settlers into the Great Plains. Grierson's men also built a considerable part of the region's telegraphic network, and Fort Sill, in Oklahoma. But they were also involved in direct combat with various Indian tribes, including the Cheyenne, Comanche, and

Above: The Buffalo Soldiers served cheerfully in a variety of roles. This troop is guarding Yosemite National Park around the turn of the 20th century.

Arapaho, and supported Sherman's winter campaigns of 1867 and 1868.

In 1875, the regiment was moved to Fort Concho in Texas. This was a return to their former role in the area: protecting the state's infrastructure, scouting unmapped territory, opening up new roads, and extending the telegraphic network. In other words, their job was to help civilize and tame this new territory, making it suitable for settlement. They were also the main law enforcers in the area, controlling outlaws, Indians, and Mexican revolutionaries.

Between 1879 and 1880, the Tenth was heavily involved in the Apache Wars, especially against the warriors of Apache chief Victorio, a violent protégé of Geronimo who was credited with the Alma Massacre of several settlers in April 1880. The regiment's most notable engagements took place at Tinaja de las Palmas and Rattlesnake Springs. They forced Victorio to retreat into Mexico, where he was finally killed by Mexican troops on October 14, 1880.

Despite the harsh discipline and conditions to which the men of the Tenth Cavalry were subjected, the regiment had the lowest desertion rate in the United States Army. The general level of desertion was extremely high at this time (in 1868, it stood at around twenty-five percent), but desertion was four times higher in white regiments than among the Buffalo Soldiers. Alcoholism was also much less common in black regiments.

Above: Victorio was the chief of the Chihenne band of the Chiricahua Apaches. He died on October 14, 1880.

Opposite page: A private from one of the six U.S. colored cavalry regiments raised by the Union to fight in the Civil War.

The Taming of Texas

Above: Stephen Austin recruited ten good men to protect the new territory of Texas. They were the nucleus of the Texas Rangers.

From their earliest days, the Texas Rangers were surrounded by the mystique of the Old West. Their role in the taming of the hugely important state of Texas cannot be underestimated, and they were the closest thing to an official police force in the West. The service countered threats from wherever they arose: villains, insurgents, Indians, and bandits. It was dangerous work, and thirty Rangers fell in the line of duty during the years 1858 to 1901. By enforcing the law of the United States in Texas, the Rangers effectively brought the state into the Union, where it would become a crucial element in the culture and economy of the West. Today, the historical importance and symbolism of the Texas Rangers is such that they are protected by statute from being disbanded.

The origins of the Texas Rangers stretch back to the earliest days of European settlement in Texas, and the organization is now the oldest law enforcement agency in North America with statewide jurisdiction. At the beginning of the nineteenth century, Mexico controlled the territory of Texas. The entrepreneurial Moses Austin was keen to encourage settlement of the state, and petitioned Texas governor Antonio Maria Martinez to allow three hundred settlers into the region. Ultimately, permission was granted. Moses died in 1821, but his son Stephen put his father's plan into action. But Texas's Mexican rulers soon proved to be unable or unwilling, to protect the incomers from Indian attack. To counter the problem, Stephen Austin recruited a fledgling force of ten men in 1823, "to act as rangers for the common defense."

For the time, the idea was revolutionary, as contemporary law enforcement in the West was, at best, patchy and informal. Austen's original force of "ranging" law enforcers is credited as the forebear of the contemporary Texas Rangers. They went on to become not only an effective force for law enforcement, but also a focus of

Western values. They "ranged" the length and breadth of the new colony, protecting white settlers from attack by several Indian tribes, including the Comanche, Karankawa, Waco, Tehuacani, and Tonkawa. When no threat was apparent, the men were allowed to return to their own land and families.

A corps of professional, full-time Rangers was established a few years later. These men were paid $1.25 a day for "pay, rations, clothing, and horse service". In this way, the men were responsible for providing their own arms, mounts, and equipment. Rangers also had to buy their own weapons, and many carried examples of the newly-introduced Colt revolving pistols. Samuel Colt had founded the Colt Manufacturing Company in 1836, in Hartford, Connecticut.

Fewer than a thousand colonists had made it to Texas by 1821 (before the involvement of the Austins). But despite attempts by the Mexican government to

Above: The Gonzales Ranging Company of Mounted Volunteers was the only fighting force to answer Colonel Travis's desperate pleas for assistance in defending The Alamo from over five thousand Mexican troops.

limit the number of American settlers, an estimated fifty thousand arrived between 1823 and 1836. Inevitably, this led to a schism of opposing interests opening up between the new American Texans and the government of Mexico. This ill feeling led to the wrongful imprisonment of Stephen F. Austin for over two years in Mexico City. He had been accused of "inciting revolution" against the Mexican regime, when he was actually negotiating for improved rights for the American settlers. Unsurprisingly, this dreadful experience converted Austin (who was to become the "Father of Texas") into a fervent believer in Texan independence. He went on to become a volunteer commander in the Texas Revolution.

When a provisional "rebel" Texan government, (known as the Permanent Council) was established by the Consultation of 1835, one of its first acts was to recruit twenty-five professional Rangers under the command of Silas M. Parker. Their primary duty was to range the frontier between Brazos and the Trinity. This force grew to three companies of fifty-six men, each commanded by a captain supported by first and second lieutenants. The three companies were commanded by a major.

Texan unrest flared into armed conflict on October 2, 1835, at the Battle of Gonzales. The Texas Revolution had begun. Hostilities raged for the following three months, until the Texan forces had defeated the Mexican troops in the region. On March 2, 1836, the Texans issued the Texas Declaration of Independence, effectively creating the Republic of Texas.

But as far as the Mexican government was concerned, the Texans were rebels who needed to be crushed. In early 1836, General Santa Anna led six thousand troops across the Rio Grande into the state. Many Texans fled to avoid his forces in what became known as the "Runaway Scrape." The Tumlinson Rangers fought a famous rearguard action to protect the shattered Texan army as it retreated, enabling it to re-group later, while other Rangers served as scouts for the Texan cause.

Buoyed by his success, Santa Anna headed towards the Alamo Mission. After a thirteen-day siege, his forces finally overcame the two hundred Texans who were defending the Mission. Every single Texan defender was killed, including James Bowie (inventor of the Bowie knife) and Davy Crockett. Santa Anna's army then swept on towards modern-day Houston. But by this time, many more settlers had joined the Texan army, now commanded by General Sam Houston. Houston's men were ultimately victorious at the Battle of San Jacinto, and Santa Anna was captured. He was forced to sign the Treaties of Velasco, which ended the war and granted

Texas its independence from Mexico. "The Last Stand" at the Alamo became a potent symbol of American resistance to foreign domination and was instrumental in Texas joining the Union in 1845.

Opposite page: A buckskin-clad Texas Ranger from the early years of the service.

In the heat of the revolution, Texans had served as both soldiers and Rangers. Some Rangers were drafted into cavalry regiments, where they were called dragoons. The Gonzales Ranging Company of Mounted Volunteers, for example, was the only fighting force to answer Colonel Travis's desperate plea for assistance in defending the Alamo from the overwhelming Mexican forces. The Rangers died heroically alongside the other defenders. Several other Rangers had been captured by General Santa Anna on his way to Houston, and were among the three hundred and fifty people that he ordered to be slaughtered on Palm Sunday 1836, in fields just outside Goliad. Sam Houston's battle cry at San Jacinto had been, "Remember the Alamo, Remember Goliad." Several individual Rangers were also noted for the contributions they made during the war, including Jack Hays, Ben McCulloch, Samuel Walker, and "Bigfoot" Wallace.

The Rangers had played a critical role in achieving Texan victory, and the service gained a great deal of recognition after independence. Government investment meant that Service also became much better equipped. In 1839, the Rangers became the first civilian force to be armed with Colts. Texas bought one-hundred and eighty Colt Patterson No. 5 Holster Model revolving pistols to arm the force. Samuel Colt had patented the gun's revolving mechanism in 1835. The weapon became known as the Texas Patterson. Samuel Walker, a Ranger who rode with Captain Jack Hays, wrote to Samuel Colt, "The pistols which you made... have been in use by the Rangers for three years... In the summer of 1844, Col. J. Hays with fifteen men fought about eighty Camanche [*sic*] Indians, boldly attacking them on their own ground, killing and wounding about half their number... Without your pistols, we would not have had the confidence to have undertaken such daring adventures."

Ultimately, the Rangers' frontier patrols were instrumental in establishing the current border between the United States and Mexico, although there were continual skirmishes along the Rio Grande for the next ten years. The Rangers continued to make punitive strikes in Mexico into the twentieth century. In one 1917 battle, it is thought that the Rangers may have killed as many as twenty Mexicans. Despite this, ethnic Mexicans and Native Americans have both become members of the Rangers Service. An Indian nicknamed Bravo Too Much rode with the most famous early Ranger, Jack Hays, in the 1830s.

Above: Jack Ford led the Texas Rangers in pursuit of the notorious Mexican-American renegade Juan Cortina.

Although Texan independence had been achieved, the work of the Rangers was far from over. The state still needed protection from Indian attack, and the rule of law needed to be established. The Rangers proved to be a cost-effective way of achieving both of these aims. Their role became more internal, and although they had been known as "los diablos Tejanos" (The Texas Devils) for their effectiveness against Mexican guerrillas, the responsibility for defending the international border was gradually devolved upon the United States army.

The next great conflict in which the Rangers were involved was the Civil War. Many enlisted in "Terry's Texas Rangers." Commanded by the brilliant Colonel E. Terry, the Rangers became part of the Army of Tennessee between 1861 and 1865, and were a great boost to the strength of the Confederate Army.

In the postbellum period of Reconstruction, the role of the Rangers was assumed by the highly political and widely disliked Texas State Police, who were charged with the implementation of the deeply unpopular "carpetbagger" laws. This force was seen as an instrument of the Union, and was highly unpopular with Texans. When Governor Richard Coke was elected in 1873, one of his first acts was to re-commission Texas Rangers. In 1874, the Texas Legislature ordered the formation of two Ranger forces. These were the Frontier Battalion, led by Major John B. Jones, and the Special Force, led by Captain Leander

McNelly. Their formation was to herald one of the most successful periods in the history of the service.

The legislation of 1874 was a defining moment in the history of the service. Rangers became officers of the peace, rather than fighting men serving in a semi-military organization, and their authority was acknowledged state-wide.

Although victory in the Texas Revolution had secured the state's international boundaries, the upheaval of the Civil War had led to a surge in internal lawlessness. The Rangers developed their role as law enforcers while continuing their fight against insurgents. They effectively neutralized the formerly powerful Comanche, Kiowa, and Apache tribes by succeeding in famous skirmishes such as the Battle of Plum Creek. The new Rangers also brought over three thousand Texan desperados to justice, including the train robber Sam Bass in 1878 and the sadistic gunfighter John Wesley Hardin. Hardin was reputed to have killed thirty-one men, but legend has it that he was captured single-handed by Ranger John B. Armstrong. Armstrong attacked him, wielding a long-barrelled Colt .45, shouting "Texas, by God!" Armstrong's hat was pierced by a bullet, but he was uninjured.

Effectively, the Rangers brought Texas under control from internal lawlessness and external threat. This made it possible for law-abiding settlers to make the state their home, and enabled Texas to become an extremely important region of the American West.

Above: This anonymous daguerreotype portrait is believed to be the only one showing a Texas Ranger wearing full battle dress.

Remington Rolling Block Rifle

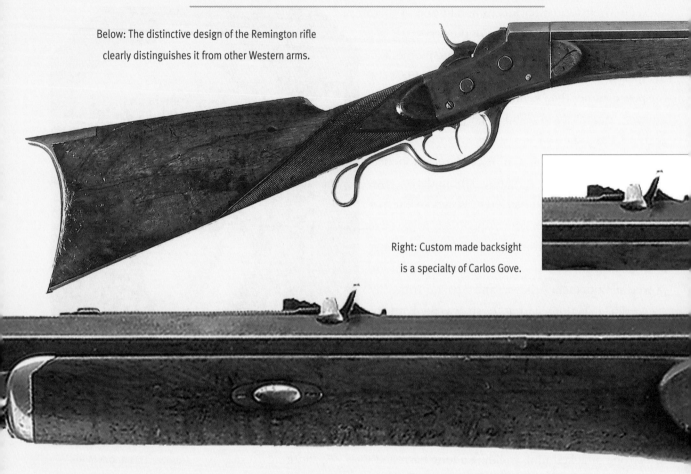

Below: The distinctive design of the Remington rifle clearly distinguishes it from other Western arms.

Right: Custom made backsight is a specialty of Carlos Gove.

Lieutenant Colonel George Armstrong Custer was one of the larger than life characters of the West. Western novelist Louis L'Amour tells us how Custer's troops cleaned up towns like Fargo-in-the Timber, "Destroying local villains like Jack O 'Neil."

Custer's time on the frontier with the US Cavalry was not just spent quelling Indians. He also took time off to go hunting in Yellowstone National Park, where he used his favorite weapon, a Remington Rolling Block Sporting rifle. In a letter written to the Remington Company on October 5th 1873 from his base at Fort Abraham Lincoln, Custer claimed that he killed far more game than all the other professional shots on the trip.

It is easy to think of rifles like the Winchester 1873 as the standard equipment for Western shots, but the Rolling Block rifle also made its mark. In the years following the Civil War, Remington

SPECIFICATIONS

Caliber: 0.40-.70 inch

Length of barrel: 30 inches

Barrel shape: Octagonal

Finish: Blue casehardened

Grips: Walnut

Action: Single shot/breech loading

Year of manufacture: 1874

Manufacturer: Remington/C. Gove & Co., Denver Armory, 340 Blake Street, Denver, Colorada

was preoccupied with chasing lucrative military contracts, but many rifles were also sold to sportsmen and hunters. They were generally used for larger game, where a powerful, large-caliber weapon was required. "The Remington system" as it was correctly known, was developed by Joseph Rider as an improvement to his split-breech concept, which was used on war models. The gun was a single-shot breech-loader that would take a heavy charge center-fire cartridge, based

on the design of army sharpshooter Colonel Hiram Berdan. Ultimately, however, the US Army decided in favor of rifles with the Allin 'trap door' action. This was a cheaper option, as Allin was a government employee and the government could avoid paying a royalty to use the system.

But the US Navy did order significant quantities of Rolling Block rifles and carbines, and this contributed greatly to Remington's success. The company must have been particularly pleased when a famed western hero and serving soldier like Custer praised their products.

Our featured gun has been converted to under-lever action by Carlos Gove, the pioneer gun-maker of Denver, and has double-set triggers. Carlos Gove rebuilt guns using this technique from 1873-77. The gun was handed down through a Western family for several generations, having been given to Charlie Robbie, the original owner, for killing an Indian at the Sand Creek Massacre.

Below: Checkered stock and double-set trigger show that this was a real shooter's gun.

The Wagon Train

Opposite page: Children formed a large percentage of the pioneers that made their way to the West. Many died on the journey from disease and accidents.

The territory of America was hugely enlarged in the first half of the nineteenth century. Jefferson's 1803 Louisiana Purchase of the land between the Mississippi and the Rocky Mountains River for fifteen million dollars was quickly followed by the acquisition of Oregon (1821), Texas (1845), and a large chunk of the West in 1848. This consisted of California, Nevada, Utah, Arizona, New Mexico, and part of Colorado. Alaska was bought from Russia in 1867. This expansion of American territory opened up great opportunities for settlement in the lands to the West, and inspired the "Great Migration" across the Rockies. This was to become the greatest mass relocation in American history. A steady flow of wagons, carts, and carriages left the eastern states across a network of trails; the Bozeman, Oregon, California, Mormon, Santa Fe, and Applegate. The two thousand-mile long Oregon and California trails were perhaps the best-trodden. In the nineteenth century, over two hundred thousand pioneers followed this route. The first trickle of westward emigration over this land route began in 1841, when fifty-eight settlers set out westwards.

Newspaper editor John O'Sullivan described this phenomenon as America's "Manifest Destiny, to overspread the continent."

Right: Many pioneers travelled to the West in trains of covered wagons. They banded together for safety and mutual assistance.

Before the Gold Rush, most westward emigration was motivated by the desire for freedom and farmland. According to English settler George Fromer, there was "good land dog-cheap everywhere" in the West. Under the Homestead Act of 1862, settlers were allowed to claim one-hundred and sixty acres for around ten dollars if they settled the land for at least five years.

Above and opposite page: These two images provide a stark contrast between a romantic view of the Western wilderness, and the reality of the harsh terrain.

Before they trekked west, most immigrants sold everything they owned – farms, animals, and household goods – to invest the money in their new life. Most were farmers, while some were artisans. James Marshall's discovery of gold at Sutter's Mill on January 24, 1848, was also a great stimulus to the westward diaspora, motivating more than eighty thousand people to hit the trails. Most of these were

Right: Most wagon trains consisted of between forty and fifty wagons. These are being drawn by oxen.

Above: Freezing accounted for around five per cent of emigrant deaths on the trail. The winter of 1856 was notoriously harsh.

single men, but some women insisted on accompanying their husbands, preferring the hardships of the trail to becoming "Gold Rush widows." Many disappointed gold seekers decided to stay in the West, and reverted to being either farmers or ranchers.

The Mormons also made up a large proportion of the westward emigrants. They first proclaimed their intention to "send out into the western country… a company of pioneers" in January 1846. By 1860, of the forty thousand white settlers in Utah, almost all were Mormons. When the railroad was introduced in 1869, their numbers swelled to over eighty thousand.

Preparation for the long and arduous journey could take many weeks and months. The trekkers knew that they would pass no settlements on their way west, and needed to carry all of their requirements with them for the next four or five months. The typical pioneer's outfit consisted of one or two small farm wagons, six to ten oxen, one or two cows, food for the journey, clothing, and utensils. Heavy possessions, such as pianos, stoves, and furniture were usually shipped to the West Coast. Provisions were perhaps the most critical element of the outfit. Taking enough flour, biscuits, bacon, coffee, tea, sugar, lard, rice, beans, eggs, corn meal, and dried fruit was absolutely critical to the success of the enterprise. The settlers also packed guns, farm and carpentry tools, cooking utensils, and crop seeds. Women pioneers often oversaw the packing of the wagons that were to carry their families to the frontier. Their aptitude for this crucial task could mean the difference between life and death.

Below: Few people actually rode the unsprung wagons. They were too uncomfortable, and the extra weight took too great a toll on the draft animals. Most pioneers walked to the West.

Many trekkers also carried one of the many published trail guides, some of which were completely misleading and dangerous.

The wagons themselves were also critical to the success of the enterprise. They needed to be strong enough to haul heavy cargoes over thousands of miles of the road-less wilderness, but light enough not to tire the animals that pulled them. Most were constructed from seasoned hardwood, usually maple, hickory, or oak. Minimal iron was used to keep the weight down. The "lubrication" system for the spring-less wagons consisted of a bucket of tar and tallow dangling from the rear axle. The wagon cover was made from canvas or cotton, and it was designed to shield the wagon from rain, dust, and sun. Another important decision was the choice of draft animal: mules or oxen. Mules were stronger and faster, but unruly. Oxen needed little grazing and were extremely strong, and were the choice of approximately three-quarters of the pioneers. Whatever the pioneers' choice of animal, they became more and more valuable with every mile they covered.

Above and opposite page: The Mormon pioneers left Nauvoo, Illinois on February 4, 1846, under the leadership of Brigham Young. Their destination was the Great Salt Lake Basin in Utah. Brigham Young first reached the Great Salt Lake Valley on July 24, 1847.

Once on the trail, life was very tough. Treasured personal possessions that had been packed with loving care were often discarded along the trail, and many travelers lost their children or spouses on the journey. Their pathetic graves were often marked only with unnamed headstones. Pioneers died from a variety of causes, accidents, and diseases. The single greatest cause of accidental death was being run over by wagon wheels. Children were especially vulnerable. Accidental shootings were also common. Other deaths were caused by fights between emigrants, lightning, grassfires, snakebites, hail storms, and even suicide.

Opposite page, above: An early photograph of Salt Lake City.

Opposite page, below: Brigham Young established way stations like Cove Fort, Utah to provide shelter to the Mormon pioneers on their way west.

Below: Around ten percent of the Mormon pioneers made their way to Utah pushing a handcart. Lacking the funds for ox or horse teams, over three thousand pioneers joined ten handcart companies.

Disease was also a serious issue on the trail. Cholera was common, and usually fatal. A person could sicken and die in just a few hours, to be buried at the trailside. Smallpox, flu, mumps, measles, and tuberculosis were highly contagious and could wipe out an entire wagon camp.

Indian attacks weren't too much of a problem for the early pioneers, as most Indian tribes were tolerant towards the pioneer wagon trains. Some even traded with the white settlers. It is estimated that only three hundred and sixty-two emigrants were killed by Indians in the years between 1840 and 1860 (while emigrants had killed four hundred and twenty-six Indians). There was much more tension in later years, when the decimation of the buffalo herds left the tribes bitter and hungry.

It is estimated that at least a tenth of the pioneers that set out on the Oregon Trail died on the way west, so there were at least twenty thousand deaths en route. Most were buried at the side of the trail with unmarked headstones.

Camp life soon became routine on the long journey. Typically, a bugler blew a trumpet at four to wake the camp. The pioneers would then round up their cattle and fixed a breakfast of bacon, corn porridge, or "Johnny cakes" made from flour and water. Everything was then packed, and a trumpeter signaled a "Wagons Ho" to start the journey. With a single rest at noon, the wagons kept rolling along the

Right: An abandoned prairie schooner. Wagon productions greatly increased with migration to the West. In the mid-1800s, Studebaker advertized that they turned out a new wagon every seven minutes. Hugely important to so many pioneer families, wagons became one of the most evocative symbols of the American West.

Above: *The Wagons,* painted by Charles M. Russell (1865-1926). A group of Native American braves watch the dust cloud raised by a faraway wagon train.

trail until evening fell. The families then ate supper and settled down for the night. Even in the extremely difficult circumstances of the trail, pioneer women were still expected to discharge their housekeeping duties. Hampered by their long skirts and impractical equipment, the simplest task became extremely arduous. One women pioneer, Lodisa Frizzel, described how tough it was: "All our work here requires stooping. Not having tables, chairs, or anything. It is very hard on the back." Another traveler, Helen Carpenter, complained about the monotony of the trail diet. "One does like a change, and about the only change we have from bread and bacon is bacon and bread."

The harsh journey took its toll on the pioneers. Miriam Davis described how she could hardly recognize herself at the end of it. "I have cooked so much in the sun and smoke that I hardly know who I am and when I look into the little looking glass ask, 'Can this be me?'"

Below: A pioneer family poses by their overturned wagon in east Oregon. They are accompanied by their black servant.

Boomers, Sooners, and Moonshiners

Above: President Abraham Lincoln.

Right: The Land Claims Office at Round Point, Oklahoma Territory, in January 1894.

Over a period of less that a century, the rush to settle the West meant that only a few areas of virgin land survived until the mid-1880s. By this time, Indian Territory had become the final frontier. Although more than fifty-five Native American tribes occupied parts of this designated territory to the west of the Mississippi, the vast majority of the land was uninhabited. This huge area was called the Oklahoma District. *Harper's Weekly* described it as "the last barrier of savagery in the United States."

President Abraham Lincoln signed the original Homestead Act on May 20, 1862. The act stated that any settler could claim one hundred and sixty acres of undeveloped federal land. The army became involved, clearing the land of illegal squatters, and organized the first great land run on April 22, 1889. This was supposed to give every settler an equal opportunity to claim the best land of the Oklahoma District. As the bugles blew at precisely noon on that day, over 100,000 "Boomers" cycled, rode trains, and drove wagons into the territory. Unfortunately, these fair-minded individuals were in many cases pre-empted by the so-called "Sooners," who had already sneaked into the Oklahoma District and

Right: Men from Troop C of the Fifth U.S. Cavalry, photographed with squatters they arrested in Indian Territory (before the area became Oklahoma).

Below: The first blacksmith shop in Guthrie, Oklahoma Territory, circa 1889.

claimed some of the best plots. The unscrupulous Sooners were often deputy marshals, surveyors, or railroad workers whose work had given them access to the district and an opportunity to study the land.

A third category of settlers, the "Moonshiners," also jumped the gun, sneaking through the lines of soldiers to get onto the territory by the light of the moon.

By nightfall on April 22, an amazing 1.92 million acres of the Unassigned Lands had been claimed. At the same time, Guthrie, which was to become Oklahoma's first state capital, was already a tent city of fifteen thousand. Within five days of the land run, the first wooden buildings were already being raised in the town. By September that year, Guthrie had three newspapers, a hotel, three general stores, and fifty saloons. Across the territory, everything necessary for civilized life sprang up almost at once. Tradesmen established their businesses, and three men set up a bank with money they had printed themselves. They used a potbellied stove as their vault.

Within weeks, the Oklahoma District was scattered with embryonic new cities, including Oklahoma City, Stillwater, Norman, and Kingfisher. Under the Organic

Overleaf: The clerical workers of the U.S. Lane Office at Perry, Oklahoma, photographed with the area's U.S. deputy marshals on October 12, 1893.

Perry, Okl

Clerical force

J. T.   U S Land Office   Oct 12,

TERSON
H MAKER
DRUG STORE

U. S. Debuty Marshal

Opposite page, top: W. H. McCoy's land claim at Perry, Oklahoma Territory. He is photographed with his friends and servants on October 1, 1893.

Act of 1890, the Oklahoma District became the Oklahoma Territory. Further land rushes opened up more and more land to settlement, although the land was now allocated by ballot. The largest of these took place in 1893, when the six million-acre Cherokee Outlet was distributed among a hundred thousand new settlers. This strip of land was fifty-seven miles wide and contained six million acres of some of the best land that the U.S. government ever offered to its settlers. The land grab began the instant that a pistol shot rang out on September 16, 1893. The treeless plains were instantly filled with the turmoil of thousands of thundering wagons, driven by dust-encrusted Boomers sweeping towards the town of Perry. The fastest run into the territory is attributed to Jack Teamey, a tax collector from Guthrie. He

Above: Hell's Half Acre, Perry, Oklahoma Territory. The tent town was photographed in 1893.

Opposite page, bottom: The Wild West Hotel on Calamity Avenue in Perry, Oklahoma Territory. The photograph was taken in September 1893.

made it from the county line (just north of Orlando) to Perry in thirty-one minutes. By four o'clock the same afternoon, he was serving beer at his new enterprise, a tent saloon called the Blue Bell. Beer was sold at a dollar a bottle, and it is reputed that over thirty-eight thousand glasses were drunk after the thirsty work of the day. Perry's recreational district, which soon became known as Hell's Half-Acre soon had no fewer than a hundred and ten saloons and gambling houses.

It was not until November 16, 1907, that Oklahoma became a state in its own right, when President Theodore Roosevelt signed a proclamation to that effect.

In the early twentieth century, the discovery of "black gold" in the state led to a great influx of wealth, and many of Oklahoma's most prestigious families made their fortunes at this time.

Left: Temporary banks and an early lodging house in Perry, Oklahoma Territory.

Colt 1882 Sheriff's (Storekeeper's) revolver

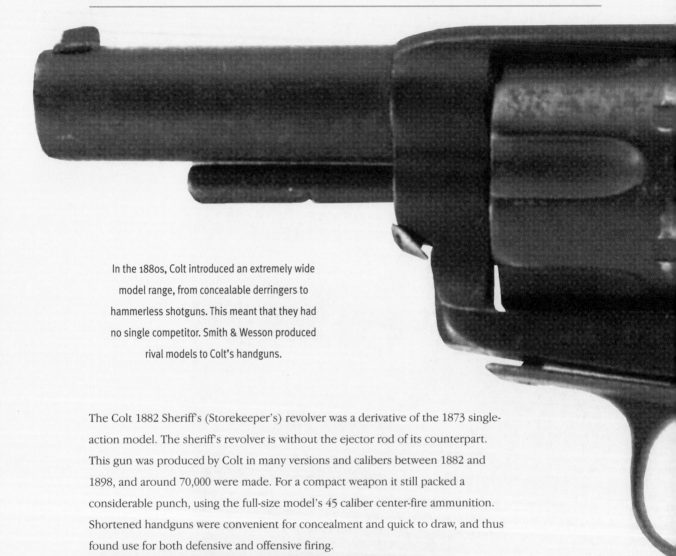

In the 1880s, Colt introduced an extremely wide model range, from concealable derringers to hammerless shotguns. This meant that they had no single competitor. Smith & Wesson produced rival models to Colt's handguns.

The Colt 1882 Sheriff's (Storekeeper's) revolver was a derivative of the 1873 single-action model. The sheriff's revolver is without the ejector rod of its counterpart. This gun was produced by Colt in many versions and calibers between 1882 and 1898, and around 70,000 were made. For a compact weapon it still packed a considerable punch, using the full-size model's 45 caliber center-fire ammunition. Shortened handguns were convenient for concealment and quick to draw, and thus found use for both defensive and offensive firing.

Left: A genuine early example of the gun, with a good original finish, can be worth $30,000.

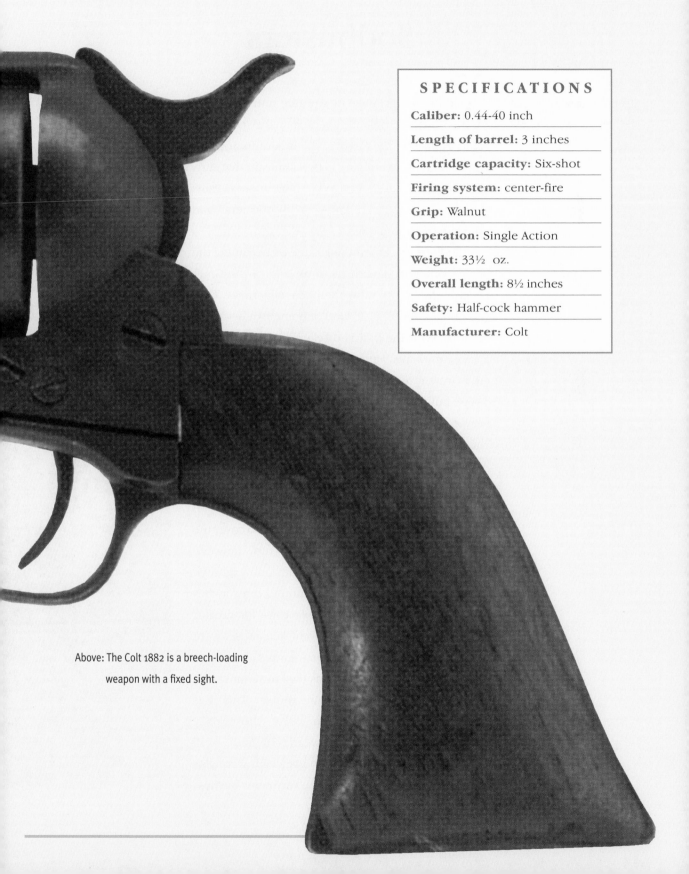

SPECIFICATIONS

Caliber: 0.44-40 inch

Length of barrel: 3 inches

Cartridge capacity: Six-shot

Firing system: center-fire

Grip: Walnut

Operation: Single Action

Weight: 33½ oz.

Overall length: 8½ inches

Safety: Half-cock hammer

Manufacturer: Colt

Above: The Colt 1882 is a breech-loading
weapon with a fixed sight.

Sodbusters

Right: This family's prairie shelter is roofed with grass turfs.

Although our image of a prairie home tends to consist of a romantic log cabin in the style of the *Little House on the Prairie*, the lack of indigenous timber and other building materials meant that early frontier settlers were obliged to build more organic structures. These were known as "sodbusters," and so were their occupants.

Sodbusters earned their name by becoming the first farmers to disturb the grassland of the Great Prairie; the first to plow the open wilderness. They also built a very special kind of home that became a nickname for the prairie-dwellers later. These early prairie dwellings were made from the virgin turf of the Great Plains itself. Some of these "sodbusters" were built into banks and hillsides, "dug in like coyotes," as one woman homesteader described it, but others were freestanding.

In the construction of these unusual homesteads, only the window frames and doors were made using timber. The walls were raised with buffalo grass sods, which were also used to cover the roof. The sods were strips of prairie turf, between twelve and eighteen inches wide, and eighteen inches long. They were usually around three inches deep. They were laid in double rows for greater strength. Even the newcomers' chicken houses were built with these materials. Many settlers also built a "cave" to keep their provisions cool in summer and stop them from freezing in winter. This was particularly important in an area whose daily temperature fluctuates between -30 and +110 degrees Fahrenheit. The sod homesteads were also thermally efficient, and could be very comfortable.

Opposite page: The interior of a large log cabin provides a warm and sociable indoor space.

With an annual rainfall of just fifteen inches, it was very hard to grow grain on the prairie, and the sodbusters' 160-acre plots provided enough grazing for only eight cows. Despite this, many settlers fell in love with the wonderful landscape of the Badlands and their peaceful lives there, with just prairie dogs and gophers for company.

Sod homes may have been the first residences of the new settlers, but the coming of the railroad meant that conventional building materials could be shipped into the area. At this time, many sodbusters were replaced by log cabins. But timber

Right: The first log cabins provided speedy shelter on the frontier, but many were comfortable and homey inside.

remained a scarce and expensive resource on the virtually treeless plains. Homesteaders still had to haul logs for many miles from railheads, or from isolated groves of hardwood trees.

Settlers that managed to acquire enough elm and cottonwood logs used them to build extremely practical and adaptable structures, which could be extended when necessary. The logs were notched at the corners to make rigid boxes, and "chinking" between the logs provided insulation. The chinking consisted of thin strips of wood which were pushed into the gaps between the logs and covered with a daub of earth and prairie grass. Cabin roofs were made from hand-split red oak or cedar shakes. Some of these log cabins were even whitewashed. But the continued scarcity of materials meant that most prairie cabins were much smaller than those in other areas. Typically, they measured just sixteen by eighteen feet,

Left: This cabin shows details of the corner joints, where the logs are neatly squared off, and the chinking used to fill any gaps between the logs. This home has an extra half-story, which was probably used for sleeping.

Right: Early settlers were known as sodbusters because they were the first to plow the virgin prairie turf. John Deere made his name by designing the first non-sticking steel plow in 1836, which turned the prairie sod into a fertile growing medium.

Below: This cabin is built from completely unshaped logs, but they fit together snugly.

and were built facing south, to catch the warmth of the sun.

The ongoing timber shortage ensured the popularity of the next building method introduced to the plains: framing. Frame homes used far less wood than log cabins, and were both sturdier and more weather proof. They were also simple

to build, as they required no foundations, and they proved to be extremely durable.

Plains homes representative of all three building methods survive today, and many have been preserved. Some of the early homes are still occupied, giving shelter to modern plainsmen and women.

Western Towns

The look and feel of Old Western towns is so completely familiar to us that we can easily imagine walking down the dusty boardwalk and through a pair of swing doors into the saloon. The classic frontier town looks flimsy, like an ephemeral movie set, and the insubstantial, flat-fronted buildings have a wonderful cinematic quality.

Real Western towns usually started as one-street settlements, with hitching rails in front of the buildings. In the early days, this main thoroughfare would be lined with archetypal Western institutions: saloons, trading posts, sheriffs' offices, livery stables, banks, gunsmiths, and telegraph offices. As the town became more established, a Wells Fargo office, Texas Rangers' office, newspaper office, barbershop, town jail, apothecary, dentist, photographer, or hotel might also open

Above: The church formed an important focus for early Western communities.

Previous pages: Wichita, Kansas in 1871. The town consisted of a street of false-fronted wooden buildings.

for business. Many towns also catered to the more spiritual side of life by establishing a church, and every town of the Old West required its own cemetery. Some of these were soon full.

Above: A more developed Western townscape, with brick and slate-roofed buildings, but cattle still wander unchecked.

Right: The commissary at Fort Smith, Arkansas. Judge Parker lodged here for some time.

Thousands of Western towns sprang up in the region as frontier life developed. They grew up at railheads, along cattle trails, near gold fields and silver mines, and around military forts. They were often isolated and surrounded by miles of empty, threatening wilderness. From the outset, Western civilization was completely different that than of the East. The landscape was bigger, and the towns were smaller.

The early establishment of law and order was crucial to the development of

Right: The St. James Saloon in Dodge City, Kansas. The interior is typical of Western bars of the period.

Above: St. Louis, Missouri became the center of the American beer industry when John Adam Lemp established his brewery there in 1840.

these townships into permanent settle-ments. Where this proved impossible, towns were often abandoned. Towns whose water or gold ran out, or those bypassed by the railroads or cattle trails, also died out, leaving very few traces.

Life on the frontier was extremely volatile, and new arrivals searched about restlessly, looking for land and opportunity. Many new towns were founded, and abandoned just a few years later.

The saloon was often the first business opened in a Western town, and might start out as just a tent or lean-to. When it became more permanent, it often doubled as a public meetinghouse. Brown's Hole, opened in 1822 near the Wyoming-

Above: The Bijou Saloon in Round Pond, Oklahoma, photographed in 1894.

Left: Every Western main street had its saloon.

Opposite page: A typical parlor girl in a friendly pose.

Colorado-Utah border was the first drinking house that became known as a saloon. It catered to the region's fur trappers. In this male-dominated region, saloons were crucial to the early development of Western towns, which often had more than one. The prevalence of bars and drinking holes was often completely disproportionate to a town's population. Livingston, Montana, had a population of only three

Above: Crapper Jack's Dance hall in Cripple Creek, Colorado.

thousand people, but no fewer than thirty-three saloons. Saloons often served liquor (whiskey, bourbon, rye, and beer) twenty-four hours a day, and their clientele reflected a cross-section of the West's white male population. These men included cowboys, gunmen, lawmen, and gamblers. Women, Chinese, and African-Americans were unwelcome, and it was actually illegal for Indians to enter. Of course, the barring of women did not extend to the saloon girls who worked in the establishments, selling over-priced drinks to the customers and keeping them company. It is estimated that most towns provided at least one prostitute per hundred men.

Many proprietors of Western saloons were gunfighters on either side of the law. These included Wyatt Earp, Bob Ford (Jesse James's killer), Doc Holliday, and Wild Bill Hickok. Many of these men were also professional gamblers.

Left: The Western general store retailed a range of goods brought to the West by rail.

Opposite page: An elaborate whiskey decanter dating from the 1880s.

As the West became more sophisticated, saloons began to offer a variety of entertainment including fine dining, billiards, singing, dancing, and bowling. The Gold Rush meant that many more professional men (including doctors, attorneys, and precious metal specialists) whose tastes were more sophisticated, made their

Right: The cozy interior of a western general store with a range of goods for pioneer families.

way to the West. But the primary saloon pastimes continued to be drinking and gambling. Almost every saloon had a poker table, and many different card games were played. Of course, gaming often led to violence, and this regularly spilled out onto the street. A complex "bar etiquette," which governed the buying and accepting of drinks, prevailed in these drinking dens. Breeches of this unwritten code could also lead to serious trouble.

Above: Hotels reflected the increased mobility of Western life.

Equally important to every town was its general store, or trading post. Without it, it would be almost impossible for a town to get off the ground. It has often been remarked that some of the biggest fortunes made in the Old West were made not by miners or settlers, but by the tradesmen who supplied them. Depending on the location of the town, the store would stock farm supplies, mining equipment, or cowboy gear. They

Colt Lightning Storekeeper

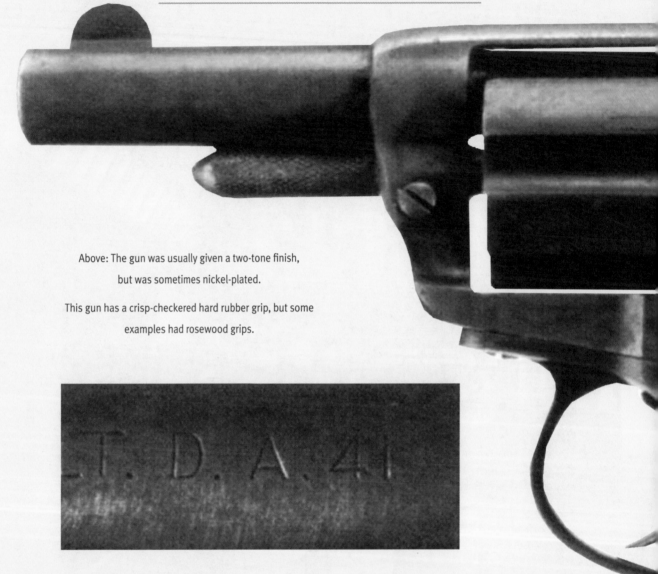

Above: The gun was usually given a two-tone finish,
but was sometimes nickel-plated.

This gun has a crisp-checkered hard rubber grip, but some
examples had rosewood grips.

A shortened revolver of the kind which became popular during the later frontier period when clothing became more Easternized. The weapons could be more easily concealed in a coat pocket or a waistband. Some were carried in purpose-made shoulder holsters by companies like H.H.Heiser of Denver. This Storekeeper model was based on the 1877 Colt Lightning double-action revolver, which quickly became popular with lawmen and gunslingers alike. John Wesley Hardin was carrying a .38 Colt Lightning revolver with a 2-inch barrel the day he was killed.

Although Colt's early attempts at double action were not flawless, the gun was quicker in getting off multiple shots –not having to be re-cocked between shots like its predecessor, the 1873 single-action.

The Colt Lightning double-action Storekeeper's model revolver came in .38 caliber, typically with a 2½-inch barrel, nickel or blued finish, and hardrubber

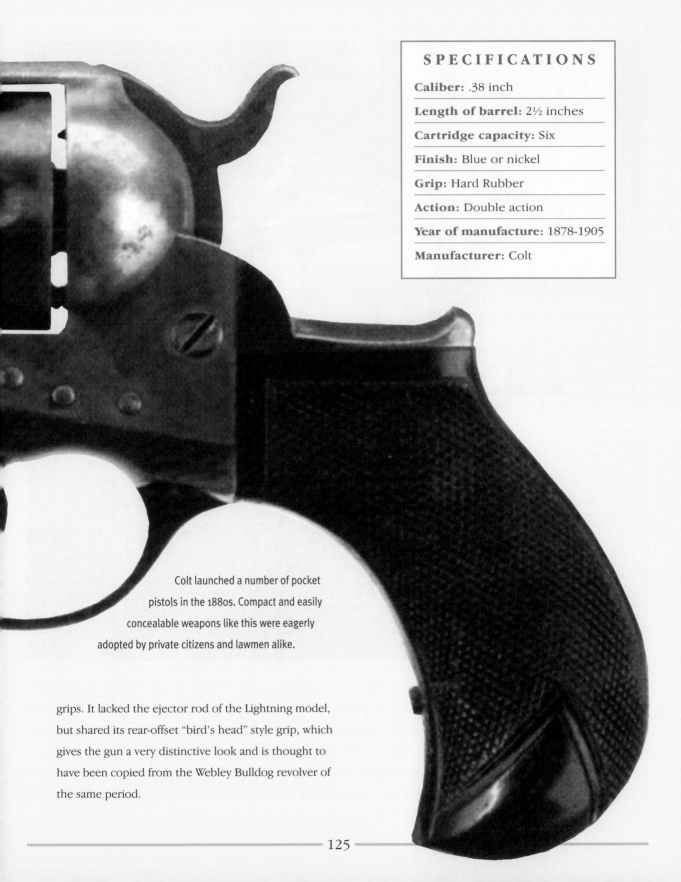

Colt launched a number of pocket pistols in the 1880s. Compact and easily concealable weapons like this were eagerly adopted by private citizens and lawmen alike.

grips. It lacked the ejector rod of the Lightning model, but shared its rear-offset "bird's head" style grip, which gives the gun a very distinctive look and is thought to have been copied from the Webley Bulldog revolver of the same period.

Above: Early Western towns were built entirely from lumber. In this sawmill, the water wheel is attached to the saw blade by a connecting rod known as a pitman arm.

also carried basic foodstuffs and seeds to get the "sodbuster" farmers started, while they prepared the prairie land to receive their crops. The general store also supplied the local townsfolk with their provisions. Perhaps the most famous Western store in popular culture is the Olesons' general store in Laura Ingalls Wilder's hometown of Walnut Grove, Minnesota. The Olesons' ambiguous social status is also interesting. While storekeepers were vital to the development of the West, many used their virtual monopolies to charge hyper-inflationary prices, and became very unpopular with their fellow townsfolk. On the other hand, many general stores and trading posts were great social centers, where news and gossip were exchanged.

As more "honest" women made their way west to join their men folk, frontier towns gradually developed the services that families needed, including medical care and education. Many well-educated young women came west to teach in the one-room schoolhouses of the region, braving loneliness and hardship to teach in very difficult conditions. Equally, many newly-qualified doctors moved west for adventure and experience, and stayed because they were so highly valued by the people of the frontier. Towns that adapted to this more "normalized" existence tended to survive, and develop a life of their own.

But after a few years of manic prosperity, many other Western towns simply disappeared from the map. The region is scattered with ghostly, abandoned settlements, whose eerie streets have not heard a footstep, or a hoofbeat, for many years.

Below and overleaf: Ghost towns and abandoned buildings litter the open spaces of the West.

Pony Express Riders

Opposite page: Frank E. Webner, the famous Pony Express rider.

Despite being one of the shortest-lived institutions of the Old West, the Pony Express has achieved a legendary status. This is undoubtedly due to the extraordinary caliber of the mail riders themselves. These men (or boys, as most of them were) have become synonymous with extreme courage, resilience, and toughness. Their spirit was the essence of the West itself. Not only did they have to counter the rigors of the trail and the dramatic weather conditions of the region, but also attacks from Indians and wild animals.

William H. Russell established the Pony Express in 1859, and set up a company with his partners William B. Waddell and Alexander Majors. His ambition was to deliver mail by an overland route from coast to coast in ten days or less, all year round. Before Russell's enterprise, mail from New York to the West travelled by steamship around South America, and this journey took at least thirty days. One of the stimuli behind the business was the start of the Civil War; Russell believed that the need for communication between the East and West was now critical. The first shipment of mail left Washington, DC by train on March 31, 1860. Three days later on April 3, a lone Pony Express rider left Pikes Peak Stables in St. Joseph, Missouri. Russell's Central Overland California and Pikes Peak Express Company used a carefully worked out route that ran for 1,966 miles between St. Joseph, Missouri, and Sacramento, California. The trail crossed plains, prairies, and deserts, and scaled mountain passes.

To make the immense journey possible, Russell established stations at approximately ten-mile intervals, employing four hundred station hands, purchasing five hundred horses, and arranging for Iowan grain to be shipped to each station. He also advertised for express riders, specifying that he wanted "young, skinny, wiry fellows not over eighteen...expert riders, willing to risk death daily. Orphans preferred." He wasn't joking, but had soon gathered the two hundred candidates he needed. Most were younger than twenty years of age and weighed less than one-

Above: Although Pony Express ceased trading in 1866, Wells Fargo retained the famous logo until 1890.

PONY EXPRESS

St. JOSEPH, MISSOURI to CALIFORNIA
in 10 days or less.

☞ **WANTED** ☜

YOUNG, SKINNY, WIRY FELLOWS

not over eighteen. Must be expert
riders, willing to risk death daily.

Orphans preferred.
Wages $25 per week.

APPLY, **PONY EXPRESS STABLES**
St. JOSEPH, MISSOURI

hundred and twenty-five pounds. For their death-defying efforts, they were paid between $100 and $150 a month.

Before they could ride for the Pony Express, each rider had to take an oath of service, stating, "I agree not to use profane language, not to get drunk, not to gamble, not to treat animals cruelly, and not to do anything else that is incompatible with the conduct of a gentleman." Each rider covered between seventy-five and a hundred miles a day at the gallop, with an average speed of ten miles per hour. They changed their mounts for fresh ones at the stations Russell had established.

Above: the Pony Express route followed the Oregon, California, and Mormon Trails and the Central Nevada Route before crossing the Sierras into California.

According to legend, John Fry was the first westbound rider, and James Randall the first to set out eastbound. Many notable Westerners rode for the Pony Express in their youth, including Wild Bill Hickok, Buffalo Bill Cody, and Calamity Jane. The service attracted, and needed, tough characters. Bronco Bill Charlie was the youngest ever Pony Express rider, signed up at the age of eleven. The oldest recruit was forty. The riders soon became an important part of Western life, charting the course of history with the documents they carried. Robert "Pony Bob" Haslam, for example, made an epic ride to deliver the news of Lincoln's election. Despite being shot through the jaw and losing three teeth, Haslam continued on his way. The service also delivered a copy of Lincoln's March 1861 Inaugural Address to Congress in a record seven days and seven hours. Bill Cody himself made the longest non-stop ride in the history of the service, when he found his relief rider had been murdered at his post. He covered three hundred and twenty-two miles non-stop, using twenty-one fresh horses. Cody's regular route was the forty-five mile stretch west of Julesburg, Colorado.

Each Pony Express rider was equipped with a specially designed mailbag, or *mochila* (taken from the Spanish word for knapsack), complete with four locked leather compartments, or *cantinas*. Each rider used the bag to carry a maximum of twenty pounds in weight, which included his personal equipment. This consisted of a water sac, a bible (courtesy of Alexander Majors), a knife, a revolver, and a horn to alert the managers of the relay stages. To save weight and ensure that the riders carried as much mail as possible, their equipment was ultimately pared down to just the water and the revolver. Originally, Pony Express mail was charged at $5 per

Opposite page: William H. Russell's recruitment poster for young riders.

Left: An abandoned Pony Express mail station at Simpson Springs in Utah's West Desert. The location bears the name of Captain James H. Simpson, a topographical engineer from nearby Camp Floyd. Simpson stopped here while laying out an overland mail route between Salt Lake City and California, attracted by the abundant water supply. The first mail station was built here in 1858. Later, it was taken over by the Pony Express.

Right: This is a mochilla. These leather covers were thrown over the saddle, and were cut to fit over the saddle horn and cantle. The mail was carried in the mochilla's four leather cantinas, or compartments.

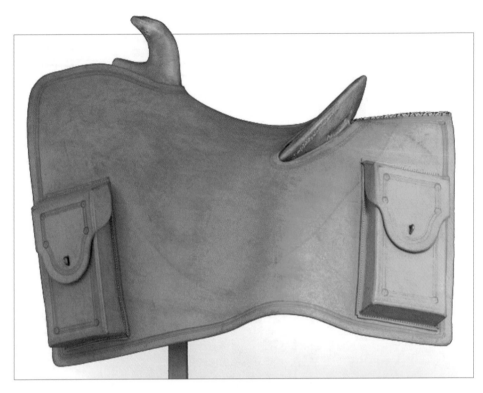

half-ounce, but to make the service more attractive, this was reduced to $2.50, and finally to $1.

Despite the high repute of the Pony Express, the company was never financially sound. Its money problems were compounded when it failed to win a one-million dollar mail contract from congress. But the final blow to the service was new technology: the telegraph. When the poles of the Creighton Telegraph Line reached Salt Lake City in October 1861, the mail service became obsolete overnight. It ceased operations two days later. The directors lost over $200,000 in the enterprise, the equivalent of millions of dollars today. Despite their entrepreneurship, two of the original Pony Express directors died in poverty. Only the God-fearing Majors made a successful new career, working for the Union Pacific Railroad. He survived until 1900.

In its short period of operation, the Pony Express riders covered over six hundred and fifty thousand miles and delivered nearly thirty-five thousand pieces of mail, with the loss of only one mailbag. A single rider had been lost, killed by an arrow shot by a Plains warrior. In 1866, the company's assets were sold to Wells Fargo Overland Mail Company for $1.5 million. Wells Fargo continued to use the Pony Express logo for its armored car service until 2001.

Despite its nineteen-month period of survival, the Pony Express had a huge impact on the West and has become an integral part of its romance. Perhaps its greatest achievement was psychological; the service broke the isolation of the Western settlers by bringing them news direct from the seat of government. It also helped keep the state of California and its gold on the side of the Union forces. Many believe that the Pony Express helped to preserve the Union itself by drawing East and West closer together, to forge one nation.

Russell's route between St. Joseph and Sacramento proved to have been very skillfully worked out, and was closely followed by the Union Pacific Railroad. The route is now shadowed by the US 36, which is known as The Pony Express Highway.

Russell's view of the West's future was also fulfilled. "The wilderness which lies between us will blossom as the rose, cities will spring into existence where the Indians and Buffalo now hold possession. Mountains will be tunneled, streams bridged and the iron monster which has become mankind's slave will ply between our confines and those far distant shores."

Below: A ruined Pony Express way station.

The Transcontinental Railway

Above: Theodore D. Judah was the chief engineer of the Central Pacific Railroad and mapped its route across the Sierra Nevada Mountains.

The building of a transcontinental railway to unite the nation was first proposed early in the nineteenth century. Ironically, the railroad became a reality just as the nation was being torn apart by civil war. Abraham Lincoln signed the Pacific Railroad Act in 1862, which set out both the route of the line and how the huge enterprise was to be financed. Lincoln firmly believed that the construction of the transcontinental line was critical to national unity. Theodore Dehone Judah, the chief engineer of the Central Pacific Railroad, had spent the summer of 1861 surveying the route the line would take. He explained the long and complicated route to the president using a ninety-foot long map. Back in 1856, Judah had written a thirteen-thousand-word proposal to build the railroad, and became a lobbyist for the Pacific Railroad Convention. He was to become one of the pivotal movers in the building of the transcontinental railroad.

The railroad was to have a huge impact on life in the West, opening it up to many more settlers. A dangerous trek that would have taken at least six months in the days of the wagon trains could now be accomplished in less than a week. But the railroad also sped up the decimation of the buffalo herds, and the annihilation of the traditional way of life of the Plains Indians.

The route of the transcontinental line followed the earlier trail routes and the Pony Express trails. It was to run between Sacramento, California, in the West and Council Bluffs, Iowa, in the East. It passed through Nevada, Utah, Wyoming, and Nebraska en route. The railway did not reach the Pacific until 1869, when a new stretch of line was opened up to Oakland Point in San Francisco Bay. The line was

integrated into the Eastern railway system until 1872, with the opening of the Union Pacific Missouri River Bridge. Its construction required tremendous engineering exploits to overcome the obstacles of the route. The line crossed several rivers (including the Platte in Nebraska), the Rockies (at the Great Divide Basin in Wyoming), and the Sierra Mountains. Spur lines were also built to service the two great cities of the Plains: Denver, Colorado, and Salt Lake City, Utah.

Above: Railway workers laid the track across the virgin land.

Right: A dramatic Currier and Ives print from 1870, entitled *Through to the Pacific*.

Opposite page: Steep-sided railway cuttings were blasted with dynamite. There were many accidents.

The Central Pacific broke ground in January 1863 on K Street in Sacramento, California, while the Union Pacific waited until December that year to start work in Omaha, Nebraska. The groundbreaking ceremonies began a monumental task that was to take six years and involve the construction of nearly two thousand miles of track. The route had to overcome many natural obstacles as the trains of the day were unable to turn around sharp curves or inclines of more than two percent. This meant that a range of innovative engineering solutions were required. This

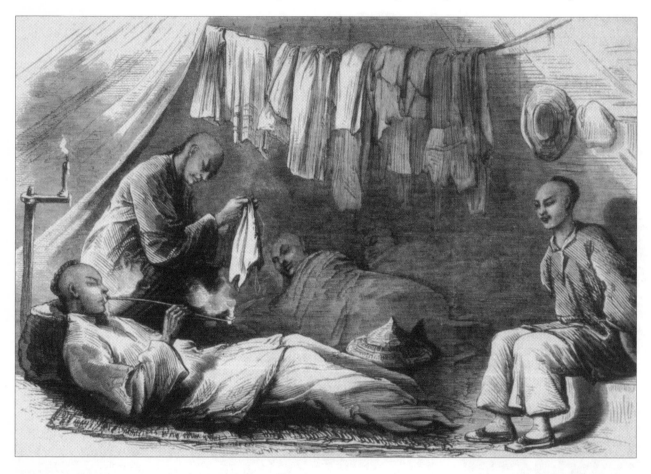

Above: Chinese railway workers constructed most of the Central Pacific track. They lived in tent towns beside the line.

enormous challenge required a massive workforce of over a hundred thousand men, who came from a wide variety of backgrounds. The majority were Irish-American veterans from both sides of the Civil War, joined by Chinese immigrants, Mexicans, Englishmen, Germans, and ex-slaves from the Southern states. Brigham Young provided Mormon workers for the Utah sector of the line. These men were excellent, conscientious workers who ended each day of work with prayer and song rather than women and drink.

Above: Construction locomotives near Bear River, Wyoming.

The project also required a wide array of professional workers, including surveyors, engineers, carpenters, masons, teamsters, tracklayers, telegraphers, spikers, bolters, and cooks.

Railway construction could be very dangerous. The use of early explosives, including unstable nitroglycerin was particularly hazardous, and resulted in many deaths and injuries. The crews from the two railroad companies were under strong competitive pressure to complete as many miles of track as possible, and their work often became sub-standard. The railway companies were paid per mile of track, not

for the durability of their construction, so their priority was speed rather than quality. Slick track-laying teams laid as many as four rails per minute. Ultimately the Union Pacific was to build about two-thirds of the transcontinental track.

Anxious not to lose a minute of working time, the railroad companies housed thousands of workers in enormous work-trains. These had sleeping cars outfitted with three-tier bunk beds, kitchens, and eating cars. The life for these men was extremely hard, and the pay meager. There were several strikes, particularly among the less well-paid Chinese workers (who were also not given room and board). But

Below: Surveyors formed the first workforce along the line, and endured many hardships. They slept on the ground, and lived in constant fear of Indian attack.

the companies were ruthless employers. They cut the food supplies to the workers, and threatened anyone who stayed away from work with punitive fines.

The two ends of the Pacific line moved slowly together, further and further into the wilderness. The workforce was spread out over several miles and was accommodated in mobile tent towns that followed the route. The end-of-line boomtowns that were created were colorful and lawless. They included North Platte, Julesburg, Abilene, Bear River, Wichita, and Dodge City. The final tent town, Corinne, Utah, was founded in January 1869. Newspaper editor Samuel Bowles coined the term "Hell on Wheels" for these mobile construction towns. They were full of vice and criminality and were rough, bawdy, and brutal. He described their

inhabitants as the "vilest men and women... (a) congregation of scum and wickedness... by day disgusting, by night dangerous. Almost everybody dirty, many filthy, and with the marks of lowest vice; averaging a murder a day, gambling, drinking, hurdy-gurdy dancing, and the vilest of sexual commerce."

Above: Triple-decker railway cars used to house the construction workers.

In reality, the tent towns mainly consisted of saloons, gambling houses, dance halls, and brothels. Almost all the women living in these settlements were prostitutes. Murder, arson, and violent crime were common. Without any real law enforcement, frontier justice was the only control, and lynching was common. John Ford captured the decadent atmosphere of Hell on Wheels in his 1924 silent film, *The Iron Horse*. Ford's movie also showed the spirit of fervent nationalism that drove this massive project. Despite their inauspicious beginnings, many of these

Right: A banner celebrates as the railroad reaches Cozad, Nebraska. The town was two-hundred and forty-seven miles from Omaha.

tent towns became permanent settlements. Mark Twain described the end-of-the-line rail town at Sacramento as a "city of saloons," but it was soon to become the state capital of California.

The railroad companies also changed the racial make-up of America by encouraging immigration from both China and Europe. The Chinese population in particular grew exponentially, from less than a hundred people in 1870 to over one-hundred and forty thousand men and women by 1880.

The companies employed agents to scout for immigrants, who were paid per head. C. B. Schmidt was the champion of scouts, responsible for settling over sixty thousand German immigrants along the route of the Santa Fe Railroad.

Another intrinsic characteristic of this huge project would be corruption. The government legislated to award the constructors with six thousand four hundred acres of trackside land, and a tiered payment per mile of track: $16,000 per mile for level track, $32,000 per mile for plateau track, and $48,000 for the most demanding stages. Within two years, these rates had been doubled. Railroad investors ensured that as much track as possible was graded into the more expensive categories. Thomas Clark Durant was one of the worst offenders. In 1864, Durant established Credit Mobilier to build the First Transcontinental Railroad track, and awarded dummy contracts to his own company. He insisted that his engineers laid the Union Pacific track in large oxbows, and tinkered with the route to ensure that it ran through his own property. His behavior became notorious, and surveyor Peter Day said that "if the geography was a little larger, I think (Durant) would order a survey round the moon and a few of the fixed stars, to see if he could not get some depot grounds." In 1867, Durant was ousted, and Congressman Oakes Ames replaced him as the head

Above: Corinne, Utah was the final tent town along the construction route.

of the organization. Ultimately, the company was revealed as fraudulent, having taken contracts worth $72 million dollars to build a railway worth only $53 million. But as railroad executive Charles Francis said, "It is very easy to speak of these men as thieves and speculators. But there was no human being, when the Union Pacific railroad was proposed, who regarded it as other than a wild-cat venture."

Union Pacific's corrupt investors became synonymous with the worst excesses of the so-called "Gilded Age." The term was coined by Mark Twain to describe the post-Civil War extravaganza of industrial-scale corruption, when massive fortunes were made and lost equally quickly. The huge volume of investment capital required to build the railroads made them especially vulnerable to speculation and sharp practice. Many railway investors were cheated and bankrupted. Oliver Jensen described these years as "the roughest age in the history of American capitalism." Many of the most magnificent San Francisco mansions were built with railroad money. The railroads were huge employers, and also provided a massive stimulus to the general economy.

On May 10, 1869, the Central Pacific and Union Pacific tracks finally met at Promontory Summit, Utah. Leland Stanford, the Governor of California and one of the "big four" investors in the Central Pacific, used a silver hammer to drive home

Below: Union Pacific director Thomas Clark "Doc" Durant stands on the advancing track in Nebraska, 1866.

Right: The *Governor Stanford* was the first of Central Pacific's twenty-three locomotives. It was photographed on its way to the joining of the rails celebrations.

the final, golden spike that joined the two lines. This was one of the world's first global media events, as both hammer and spike were wired to the telegraph line, and Stanford's ringing blows were simultaneously broadcast to the East and West Coasts of America. A signal of "Done" was sent across the country from Staten Island to the Golden Gate, and ignited a unprecedented national celebration. The dream of Manifest Destiny had finally been achieved.

The line had a great impact on the whole country, but its effects were most directly felt in the West. It proved to be a major stimulus to both immigration and trade. Charles Nordhoff described its fundamental importance: "On the plains and in the mountains, the railroad is the one great fact." Soon, other railroads crisscrossed the Plains, including the Kansas Pacific, North Pacific, Denver Pacific, Texas and Pacific, Burlington and Missouri River, Denver and Rio Grande, Atchison, Topeka, and Santa Fe railroads. By 1876 it was possible to travel between New York and San Francisco in three-and-a-half days. For most people, though, the reality of rail travel was basic and uncomfortable. In 1879, Robert Louis Stevenson described his Union Pacific train carriage as being "like a flat-roofed Noah's Ark, with a stove and a convenience, one at either end, a passage down the middle, and transverse benches upon either hand."

Settlement of the prairie led to a massive increase in American farming. The two million working farms that existed in 1860 had grown to six million by the end of the century. Westward migration corresponded with a huge influx of settlers into the United States itself; immigration from overseas doubled to over five million in the 1880's.

For the Native Americans, the coming of the

railroad was a disaster of epic proportions. The colossal increase in white settlement was one great source of anger. The other was the decimation of the American bison. This animal was unique to the Plains, and before the railroad it was estimated that as many as sixty million roamed the prairie in massive herds. The buffalo was crucial to the existence of the Plains Indians and had a special spiritual significance to them. "Everything the Kiowas had had come from the buffalo," said tribe member Old Lady Horse. "Their tepees were made of buffalo hides, so were their clothes and moccasins. They ate buffalo meat." The other Plains tribes, including the Cheyenne, Lakota, and Apache, were equally dependant on the buffalo.

But the railroad companies saw the ancient bison herds as a dangerous nuisance, useful only for the feeding of their workforce. They hired a generation of buffalo hunters to wipe them out. The most famous of these was Buffalo Bill, who worked for the Kansas Pacific Railroad. Mounted on his horse, Buckskin, and armed with his gun, Lucretia, Buffalo Bill shot over four thousand animals in less than eighteen months. He also

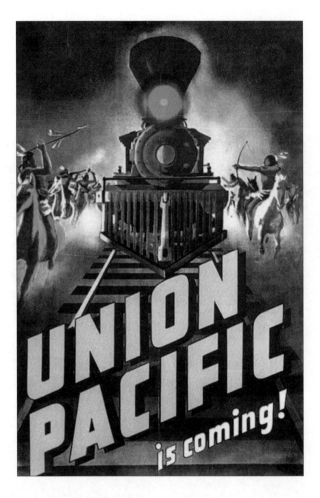

Above: Cecil B. DeMille's 1939 movie *Union Pacific* starred Barbara Stanwyck. It focused on the national unity engendered by the railroad.

Left: An emigrant ticket from Chicago to San Francisco.

Opposite page: This 1869 poster celebrates the grand opening of the railroad from the Atlantic to the Pacific.

Opposite page: Buffalo Bill worked as a buffalo hunter for the Kansas Pacific Railroad.

organized many hunting expeditions. Buffalo hunting became so popular that the railway companies encouraged their passengers to shoot buffalo from specially adapted railcars. Elisabeth Custer described how "the wild rush to the windows, and the reckless discharge of rifles and pistols put every passenger's life in jeopardy." The trend became so widespread that the Kansas Pacific Railroad ran its

Above: This dramatic Currier and Ives print shows bison swarming along the route of the railroad.

own taxidermy service to mount trophies for their customers. The result of this dreadful slaughter was that, by the end of the end of the nineteenth century, only a thousand bison survived from the majestic herds that had dominated Plains life for centuries. As Sitting Bull bitterly commented, "What is this? Is it robbery? You call us savages. What are *they*?"

Seeing their way of life being destroyed before their eyes, some of the more warlike Plains Indian tribes began to organize scouting parties to vandalize trains and attack surveyors and other railway workers. This gave the rail companies the

Left: Shooting buffalo from trains became so popular that the Kansas Pacific Railway Company established its own taxidermist to mount the passengers' trophies.

Below: Union Pacific locomotive 82 and its crew. The train was photographed in 1872 on the line between Echo, Utah and Evanston, Wyoming.

excuse they needed to strike back. According to General Grenville Mellen Dodge, the chief engineer of the Union Pacific, "We've got to clean the damn Indians out, or give up building the Union Pacific Railroad." The Sand Creek Massacre of November 1864 was one of the most appalling incidents that took place, when men of the Colorado Territory militia destroyed a village of Cheyenne and Arapaho, killing over two hundred elderly men, women, and children. Although the massacre was widely condemned, no one was brought to justice. Sand Creek led to a series of revenge killings in the Platte Valley, and over two hundred innocent white settlers were murdered. The increasing spiral of violence made it progressively more difficult for an accommodation to be found between the Plains natives and the railroad companies. The U.S. Cavalry was deployed to protect the security of the trains. Dodge ordered the Powder Ridge Expedition of 1865, in which his forces rode against the Lakota, Cheyenne, and Arapaho tribes. Although this was partly successful, hostilities soon escalated into the Red Clouds War, fought against the Lakota tribe in 1866. The Lakota braves inflicted heavy casualties in the conflict, and it was the worst defeat that the U.S. Cavalry was to suffer until Little Bighorn, ten years later.

Their resistance to the railroad led to the Plains tribes being confined in reservations, where they were powerless to protect their ancestral hunting groundsor the buffalo.

Despite the mixed heritage of the Transcontinental Railroad, its completion was an extraordinary achievement that was celebrated as an icon of Western culture. The railroad is familiar from any number of Westerns that show the great iron horses crossing the monumental Plains landscape. In 1936, Cecil B. DeMille released *Union Pacific*, which explored the corruption that surrounded the building of the line. *How the West Was Won*, John Ford's epic movie of 1962, also dealt with the dramatic construction of the Union Pacific line. The film unequivocally blames the railroad bosses for enraging the Arapaho tribe at the expense of their workers' lives.

The Transcontinental Railroad left a permanent mark on American life in both the East and West of the country. The sound of the train whistle became a haunting and romantic sound across the prairies. The line itself has been renewed many times, but much of it is still laid on the original, hand-prepared grade. In several places, where later routes have bypassed the original line, it is still possible to see the obsolete track, abandoned in the wilderness.

Above: The Central Pacific and Union Pacific tracks met on May 10, 1869.

RESUME
SPEED

C.A.F.

Left: An immaculate railroad baggage cart. Built from a standard pattern, the cart is ten feet long, forty-one inches wide, and has thirty-inch wheels. These carts were pushed by baggagemen, who loaded the goods into the baggage cars. Each railroad company painted their equipment in their livery colors.

Remington Double Derringer

The derringer was a popular choice of defensive weapon for frontier people, especially women. A derringer is defined as the smallest usable handgun of a given caliber. Derringers appealed to women because they could be easily concealed in a purse or dress pocket, or tucked into a garter. Guns that were specifically designed for female use were called "muff pistols," but Derringers were also marketed to men.

The weapon was named for Henry Deringer, a Philadelphia gunsmith who developed a range of compact, high-caliber pocket pistols that, despite their size, had reasonable stopping power. Deringer's guns were so successful that his name became synonymous with all weapons of the type. The press report of Abraham Lincoln's assassination wrongly spelt the name of John Wilkes Booth's weapon as "Derringer." This version of the gun's name fell into common usage.

Early derringers were not repeating firearms. Repeating mechanisms such as those used in semi-auto-

SPECIFICATIONS

Caliber: .41 inch Rim fire
  Cartridge

Length of barrel: 3 inches

Barrel shape: Round/ribbed

Finish: Blue steel

Grips: Hard Rubber

Action: Breech loading double
  barrel

Year of manufacture: 1870

Manufacturer: Remington
  Arms Company, Ilion,
  New York

matic handguns or revolvers would have added significant bulk and weight to the gun, defeating the purpose of these highly concealable weapons. The original cartridge derringers held only a single round. These guns were usually chambered for either single pinfire or rimfire .40 caliber cartridges. The barrel pivoted sideways on the frame to allow access to the breech for reloading. The famous Remington derringer doubled the firing capacity of the early models, while maintaining their compact size. This was achieved by adding a second barrel on top of the first. The barrels pivoted upwards to reload. Each barrel held one round, a .41 rimfire bullet, and a cam on the hammer alternated between the top and bottom barrels. Travelling at only four-hundred and twenty-five feet per second, the derringer's bullets moved slowly enough to be seen by the naked eye, but at close quarters they could be fatal. Remington sold the gun between 1866 and 1935.

Below: Even the fixing screw for the handgrip was delicately designed.

Wells Fargo

Below: The Wells Fargo offices in San Francisco.

Wells Fargo was one of the great institutions of the West, and was a positive force for the civilizing of the wild frontier. Its very name conjures a thrilling image of a six-horse stagecoach loaded with gold, thundering across the romantic landscape of the Plains. The business activities of Wells Fargo became part of the fabric of the West, serving people of every background and profession. The company also sought to control lawlessness in the region, especially along the stage routes.

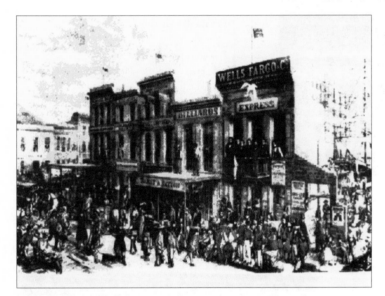

Henry Wells and William Fargo founded the company in 1852, and set up their first office at 420 Montgomery Street in downtown San Francisco. This location was in the heart of the '49ers' tent city. The new company offered financial services, and also traded in gold. Even more importantly, they also offered express, secure carriage for all kinds of cargo, especially gold dust and bullion from the area's newly sunk mines. Right from the beginning, there was a thread of altruism and impartiality in the company culture. Wells Fargo offered their services to all "men, women, or children, rich or poor, white or black." Indeed, they ran their business for all the settlers and frontier people of the West. Henry Wells was also a proponent of sexual equality, founding Wells College for Women in New York with the slogan, "Give her the opportunity!" By the 1880's, several women were Wells Fargo agents, sometimes taking over from their husbands as company employees when they were widowed. Veterans of the U.S. Army have now worked for the company for over a hundred and fifty years.

Integrity was a great factor in the success of the business and Wells Fargo agents often became highly esteemed figures in the new towns of the West. New agents were recruited from well-respected members of the community, including storekeepers and attorneys. Each was given a certificate of appointment by the company. As well as the express service, the agents also offered basic banking and financial services.

Opposite page: N.C. Wyeth's 1909 painting, *The Pay Stage*. Wells Fargo stagecoaches were usually protected by an outrider armed with a shotgun.

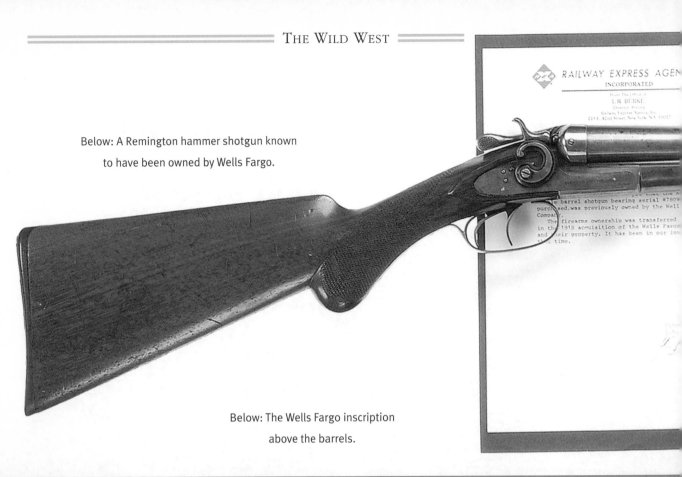

Below: A Remington hammer shotgun known
to have been owned by Wells Fargo.

Below: The Wells Fargo inscription
above the barrels.

RAILWAY EXPRESS AGENCY
INCORPORATED

From The Office of
L.R. BURKE
Director, Pricing
Railway Express Agency, Inc.
219 E. 42nd Street, New York, N.Y. 10017

...e barrel shotgun bearing serial #78096
purch sed.was previously owned by the Well...
Compa y.
     The firearms ownership was transferred
in th 1918 acquisition of the Wells Fargo
and eir property. It has been in our inv...
   time.

Left: Wells Fargo issued their operatives with recognizable badges. Their logo became a symbol of civilization coming to the West.

The company started their overland stagecoach line in the 1860's. Wells Fargo had had shares in the Butterfield Overland Mail Company established in 1858. Ultimately, Wells Fargo took the company over and used this for the basis of their mail business. The company sent the mail by the fastest means possible; stagecoach, steamship, railroad, pony rider, or telegraph. Their operatives often brought the mail through at dreadful personal risk, and it was said that the mail was delivered "by God and Wells Fargo." Wells Fargo also employed detectives to investigate fraud and any other illegal practices in connection with their

Above: The Wells Fargo stage waits for passengers outside a commercial hotel.

Opposite page: A modern-day recreation of the Wells Fargo stagecoach rattling into town.

business, and employed armed escorts and shotgun riders to discourage theft and hold ups. They were reputed to carry cut-down shotguns, which were easy to conceal under the seat of a wagon and lethal at close range. This modus operandi daunted many less serious villains, but the company did fall victim to several serious offenders. Black Bart was one of the most irksome stage robbers to victimize the company, beginning his campaign of robbery in 1875. They hired James B. Hume as their chief detective to try and stop the holdups, and he remained with the company for thirty-two years, becoming one of the most famous detectives in the country. Hume finally caught up with Black Bart after twenty-eight stage robberies. He assigned an armed guard to ride in every express car that carried mail as well as

Above: A Wells Fargo's padlock, manufactured by Ayers, Climax, and Romer. Opposite page: Madison Larkin was a Wells Fargo messenger and shotgun guard. He was photographed in Phoenix, Arizona in 1877.

Wells Fargo valuables, and posted a standing reward of $300 for information about any crimes committed against the company. Wells Fargo also became the victim of train robberies. The first big one happened in 1870 when the Central Pacific out of Oakland was held up near Truckee. Seven masked men stole $42,000 in gold.

By 1866, Wells Fargo was operating all the major overland stagecoach lines west of the Missouri, and soon drove on to Salt Lake City. Gradually, Wells Fargo took over the routes of the Pony Express. Their stages eventually rolled over three thousand miles of territory. They used stagecoaches constructed by carriage builder

A gold panning pan embossed with the Wells Fargo logo. The pan is twelve inches across.

J. Stephens Abbot and master wheelwright Lewis Downing, constructed in their Concord, New Hampshire, factory. The unique feature of the Wells Fargo coach was its suspension, which rested on bull hide leather "thorough braces." This gave the coaches a rolling gait rather than a jarring

Above: A small Wells Fargo coach, drawn by a single horse.

motion. Mark Twain accurately characterized the Wells Fargo coach as "an imposing cradle on wheels." The coaches weighed in at around two-and-a-half thousand pounds and were decked out with damask cloth interiors, which cost a substantial $1,100.

Trains became an increasingly vital part of the Wells Fargo network. By 1888, the railroad enabled Wells Fargo to offer an "Ocean-to-Ocean Service" through twenty-five different states. The company was now divided into three departments, "P" Pacific, "C" Central, and "A" Atlantic.

Wells Fargo continued to run its express business, delivering valuable cargoes of every kind, up until 1918, when it was taken over as part of the government war effort.

Acknowledgements

The Buffalo Bill Historical Center

Kansas State Historical Society

Patrick F. Hogan, Rock Island Auction Company

L.D.S. Church Archives, Museum of Church History and Art, Salt Lake City

National Cowboy Heritage Museum

Wells Fargo History Museum

J.P. Bell, Fort Smith, Arkansas

Colorado History Society

The National Archives

Kathy Weiser, Legends of America

The United States Naval Academy Museum